The Suppres~

C000215222

The Suppression of Guilt

The Israeli Media and the Reoccupation of the West Bank

Daniel Dor

Pluto Press

LONDON • ANN ARBOR, MI

First published 2005 by Pluto Press
345 Archway Road, London N6 5AA
and 839 Greene Street, Ann Arbor MI 48106

www.plutobooks.com

British Library Cataloguing in Publication Data
A catalogue record for this book is available from the British Library

ISBN 0 7453 2295 6 hardback
ISBN 0 7453 2294 8 paperback

Library of Congress Cataloging in Publication Data
Dor, Daniel, 1963–
   The suppression of guilt : the Israeli media and the reoccupation of the
West Bank / Daniel Dor.
     p. cm.
   Includes bibliographical references and index.
   ISBN 0–7453–2295–6 (hardback) — ISBN 0–7453–2294–8 (pbk.)
   1. Arab-Israeli conflict—1993—Press coverage—Israel. 2. Arab-Israeli
conflict–1993—West Bank—Press coverage—Israel. 3. Mass media—Moral
and ethical aspects—Israel. I. Title.
   DS119.76.D68 2005
   070.4'4995694054—dc22

                                                        2005001488

10   9   8   7   6   5   4   3   2   1

Designed and produced for Pluto Press by
Chase Publishing Services Ltd, Fortescue, Sidmouth, EX10 9QG, England
Typeset from disk by Stanford DTP Services, Northampton, England
Printed and bound in Canada by Transcontinental Printing

Contents

Acknowledgments

The core part of this book (chapters 3 through 5) was originally published in Hebrew, in a report commissioned by *Keshev*, the Center for the Protection of Democracy in Israel. The report was published in 2003, under the title *Behind Defensive Shield*, by *Babel Publications*. I would like to thank Yizhar Be'er from *Keshev*, and Amit Rotbard from *Babel*, for their support, cooperation and friendship. I would like to thank Miriam Hadar for her help with the translation, Jérôme Bourdon and Amit Pinchevski for reading parts of the book and offering valuable criticism, and my seminar students at Tel Aviv for their questions and comments. Many senior editors and reporters from the Israeli media agreed to meet and talk, and they offered me their frank perspectives on the complex issues raised in this book. I would like to thank them for that. Special thanks to Anne Beech and Judy Nash from *Pluto Press*, for believing in the book and for taking such good care of it. Finally, I would like to thank Lia Nirgad for her support and encouragement, for her help with the translation, for her penetrating insights, for giving me the opening sentence of the book, and, most importantly, for being the wonderful person that she is.

1
"Between the Hague and Jerusalem": An Introduction

Some stories start with an epilogue. On Monday, February 23, 2004, as this book was already well on its way, the International Court of Justice at the Hague launched its hearings on the legality of Israel's Separation Wall. For most Jewish Israelis, this was only another painful proof of the inherent hostility of the world community towards Israel, a hostility rooted in anti-Semitism, which also spelled a fundamental indifference towards Jewish suffering: on the previous morning, a Palestinian suicide bomber boarded bus No. 14 in Jerusalem and blew himself up. Eight citizens, among them two children, were killed. Dozens were wounded. The two major Israeli newspapers, *Yediot Ahronot* and *Ma'ariv*, dedicated their entire news sections on Monday morning to this dramatic contradistinction "between the Hague and Jerusalem". *Yediot Ahronot's* front-page headline was actually directed at the ICJ judges themselves:

"You Sit in Judgment – And I Bury a Husband"

Under the headline appeared an open letter from Fanny Haim, whose husband, Yehuda, was killed in the terror attack. The letter was accompanied by a picture of the couple, hugging each other, looking at the camera, with an unmistakably Dutch landscape stretching behind them – a couple of windmills in a grass field and a lake. As the caption explained, the picture was actually taken in the Hague, when the couple visited Holland a few years ago. This is what Fanny Haim said in her letter:

Today, you will sit there, in the Hague, and judge. Today, I will bury my husband, and my heart, torn into pieces. I am no politician. I address you as someone who has lost a husband, a person whose heart no longer functions – and a person whose tragedy could have been prevented by the separation fence ... Today, when you start discussing the big issues, think, if only for one moment, of the little people behind this bloody

1

struggle. Think for just one moment about my husband's good heart, or about his little son, Avner. He is only ten years old. Maybe you can try and explain to him why the hell he no longer has a father ... Do not judge my country, do not try to prevent it from preventing more victims. Today I bury a husband. Do not you bury justice.

Next to the letter appeared a commentary by Nahum Barnea, arguably the single most important journalist in the Israeli press. Under the title "When Israelis Weep", Barnea said:

Terror has cut a quick shortcut between kitsch and death: inspired by the installation created by the former Israeli Dror Feiler in Stockholm,[1] the rescue and recovery organization ZAKA[2] has decided to transport to the Hague a bus from one of the terror attacks in Jerusalem. By the time the bus arrived at the Hague and its pieces had been re-soldered, another bus exploded in Jerusalem.

Ma'ariv's perspective on that morning was practically identical. Its entire front page was covered by an enormous picture of a wounded soldier, his face covered with blood. The top banner highlighted the contradistinction of the day:

Jerusalem: 8 Murdered in a Terror Attack;
The Hague: Israel Stands Trial

The main headline, stretched across the picture in red letters, was directed not at the ICJ judges, but at the paper's own *readers*:

You Be The Judges

and the subheadline added: "The terrorist who murdered children on their way to school penetrated Israel where there was no fence. For the judges' information".

There was relatively little news in the papers on that morning, and a lot of emotion. What the two newspapers mostly did was express, reflect, impress and highlight a certain collective sensibility: a sarcastic, angry, irritated, tenacious, frightened sense of siege – a physical siege, of course, but also, and much more significantly, a *mental* siege. More than anything else, what reverberated from the papers much more than the fear, or the anger, or the mourning for the victims of the suicide attack, was the insult of *blame*.

This book tells the story of the Israeli media and their coverage of operation Defensive Shield, the largest Israeli incursion into the Palestinian territories since the outbreak of the second Intifada, but on the morning the ICJ hearings opened I thought I should open the book with their coverage. Not just because they are, in a way, the last episode in the story, as we shall see immediately, but also because they turned into reality something that hovered over the Israeli collective consciousness for a very long time, and took over the coverage of the operation itself: the desperate need to suppress, to dismiss, to fend off *guilt*. The newspapers of February 23 are the most explicit demonstration of what, in operation Defensive Shield, takes a much more complex form.

The suppression of guilt is a much wider phenomenon than the mere suppression of *information that potentially implies guilt*. The suppression of such information is of course one way to suppress guilt, but the examples we have looked at demonstrate some of the others: the accentuation of *victimhood*, for example, and the rhetorical usage of sarcasm. The papers do not suppress guilt by playing down the *information* about the ICJ trial: they highlight the hearings, and dismiss the implication of guilt by playing the hearings against the suicide attack in Jerusalem. As we shall see, guilt can also be suppressed by counter-blaming (the other side is guilty, therefore I am *not*), and by disqualifying the source of blame or the judging authority (*they* have no right to judge *me*). It can be explained away by blurring intention (I did not mean to do that, it happened by *mistake*), and by recourse to a claim about coercion (I was *forced* to do what I did). And guilt can be bluntly pushed aside in defiance (I know exactly what I did, but I don't care). We shall see examples of all these in the book; together, they give the Israeli coverage of operation Defensive Shield an unmistakable character.

The operation was launched almost two years after the outburst of the second Intifada[3] (approximately two years before the ICJ hearings), on the night of March 29, 2002, after a long month of almost daily suicide bombings, culminating in the attack on Park Hotel in Netanya, on Passover Eve, March 27. Twenty-eight people who had attended the Seder dinner at the hotel were killed. Within 24 hours, the army had issued emergency call-up notices for 20,000 reserve soldiers, the largest such call-up since the 1982 incursion into Lebanon. The next day, the tanks rolled into Ramallah, and by April 3, the Israeli Defense Forces (IDF) were conducting major military operations in most Palestinian cities. The operation, the largest of its type since the occupation of 1967, lasted for more than three weeks, and reached its most dramatic and violent point in the conquest of the Jenin refugee camp, which elicited allegations in the international press about a massacre. Rather then being suppressed, these allegations featured prominently in Israeli coverage of the events. What determined the nature of the coverage, however, was not the contents of the allegations, but the allegations themselves – the very fact that Israel was being accused of immoral and intentional behavior. Thus, just as with the ICJ hearings, the unsaid topic of coverage was the issue of guilt.

Throughout the first, crucial week of the operation, all journalists, Israeli and international, were barred from 'military' areas, which included all the major Palestinian cities. When the operation ended, the West Bank was for all practical purposes under renewed Israeli occupation, Yasser Arafat was held prisoner in his headquarters, the *muqata'a*, in Ramallah, and the Palestinian Authority was in effect dismantled. More than any other event throughout the Intifada, the operation changed the reality on the ground in the most fundamental fashion, and paved the way to the next stage of the conflict, in which Israel, having regained control of the areas it had previously withdrawn from, launched the construction of the wall – the very wall it was to stand trial for less than two years later.

This book examines the coverage of the operation by the five major Israeli news providers – the three major national newspapers, *Yediot Ahronot*, *Ma'ariv* and *Ha'aretz*, and the two major television channels, Channel 1 and Channel 2 – between March 29 and April 26 2002.[4] Chapter 2 begins with a discussion of methodology. Far from technical, it attempts to propose a novel approach to the question of *bias*, an approach which does not presuppose an objective description of reality as a standard against which media representations of reality are compared and evaluated. As I will try to show, the release of the analysis from the competition between narratives and the struggle over truth will help us develop an *intertextual* method of critical analysis, which will, in its turn, allow for a better understanding of what the essence of the bias consists of.

Chapters 3 through 5 then present the actual analysis of the coverage. Some of the questions which these chapters attempt to answer are: how do the different media present the goals and overall significance of the operation to the public? To what extent do they try to question the goals of the operation as formulated by the government? Do the different media accept the government's contention that the Palestinian Authority should be equated with the "infrastructure of terrorism"? How did they present Arafat's role in the ongoing events? To what extent do they allow for the exposition of the Palestinian perspective on the events? How do they report the IDF's activities on the ground, the results of these activities and the situation of the civilian population under renewed IDF occupation? How do they react to the IDF's closure of the territories to journalists? How do they treat the political (parliamentary and grassroots) opposition to the operation? How do they describe the public's sentiments with respect to the operation? To what extent do they take an active part in the propaganda war which took place throughout the operation, especially after the events in Jenin?

As we shall see, each of the media institutions actually offered its readers or viewers a significantly *different* perspective. These perspectives varied with respect to each of the topics mentioned above: many of them were genuinely critical with respect to some of the issues, and the picture which thus emerges makes it quite difficult to pigeonhole most of the different news providers as simply "patriotic", "liberal" or "nationalistic". What the different media did seem to share, however, beyond the factual and interpretative differences between their perspectives, was a certain emotional attitude, not *vis-à-vis* the operation itself (where they differed significantly), but with respect to the global discourse of blame against Israel.

As I will show in Chapter 5, all the different media, with virtually no exception, implicitly complied with a basic imperative: they supressed reports that could be perceived as *incriminating*, that is, reports which would suggest unreasonable or immoral acts committed by Israel *intentionally*, both at the level of government policy and at the level of IDF conduct on the ground. Most significantly, the media suppressed reports which strongly indicated that the goal of the entire operation was not the fight against terrorism, but the reoccupation of the West Bank and the destruction of the Palestinian Authority. This pattern strongly indicates that what is at stake, what lies at the heart of the matter, is the issue of guilt: all the different media found it relatively easy to admit to unreasonable acts committed by Israel (or Israelis) unintentionally, by *mistake*, but systematically supressed those where prior intention logically implied guilt.

This constant struggle against guilt goes hand in hand with a wider world-view, one which fends off guilt by *blaming the other side*. This world-view insists that Israel does not have its own agenda in the present crisis, that it was dragged into it by Palestinian terrorism, and that the occupation and the IDF's mode of operation play no role in the persistence of terror. More than anything else, it reflects the deep-seated conviction that a diplomatic solution is not viable at this point, as Israel had already done all it could in order to attain peace, and thus played no active role in the tragic deterioration of the region back into what now seems like an intractable conflict.

In the concluding chapter of this book, I will offer a few theoretical remarks, concentrating on the social role of this type of coverage. I will claim that reducing the coverage to an attempt to *manufacture consent* with the government, the military and their actions fails to capture the essential nature of the coverage, as well as its overall complexity. To be sure, some of the coverage, some of the time, results in the strengthening of consent (and some of the coverage, as we shall see, is *explicitly* about that). This, however, does not exhaust the meaning of the coverage. In operation Defensive Shield, most of the media coverage is about the proposition of different alternatives for the construction of an Israeli *identity*, different alternatives which, among other things (and not necessarily most importantly), include different attitudes towards the establishment. More than anything else, the perspectives offered by the different media are assertions about *what it should feel like to be Israeli* in the midst of all the confusing complexity which reality produces, and during operation Defensive Shield, all the different perspectives converged around one assertion: being Israeli feels mainly like being accused by the entire world, and sometimes by other Israelis, of something you are not guilty of.

In this sense, the media are doing something they have always done in modern societies, something which is not *reducible* to the maintenance of the relationship between the people and the establishment: they construct and maintain *imagined communities*. They provide their individual consumers with an implicit characterization of what the other members of their community feel and think. In other words, they *persuade* by insisting that the *other* members, the majority, are already persuaded, and thus preserve and strengthen their *own* power over the people. In operation Defensive Shield, the context of this type of persuasion is not so much the classic context of the nation-state, its interests and its structural constraints (although these, quite obviously, play a significant role), but the postmodern context of world opinion and the global media. In this context, the Israeli media functions as a *local*, rather than a *national*, institution.

It is with this understanding that the very notion of *critical analysis* should find itself a new foundation. Not with the conviction that the media necessarily manufacture consent, not in the struggle over truth and the validity of narratives, but in the understanding of the relatively independent power that the media has over people, in its ability to construct what people think about *themselves* – and in the impact of *this* on what is actually taking place in reality. Obsessed as they are with the discourse of guilt, the Israeli media effectively prevent Israeli society from developing a discourse of *responsibility*, a discourse which, regardless of the struggle over the "origins of the conflict", understands that Israel, and Israelis, have to assume responsibility for the *solution* of the conflict, because at present, in reality, the Palestinians are under Israeli occupation and not the other way around. In this, the Israeli media effectively contribute to the continuation of violence.

2
Objective Reality and Intertextual Analysis: The Definition of Bias

Critical analysis of media representations usually revolves around two questions, which are quite obviously related to each other, but are nevertheless fundamentally different. The first question is interested in the opposition between *truth* and *falsehood*: to what extent does the media provide the public with full, accurate, reasonable, well-rounded, unbiased representations of *reality*? The second question is also concerned with the notion of *truth*, but this time in its opposition with the *lie*: does the production of the news, as a social function, amount to an attempt to *manufacture consent*, to produce a certain hegemonic perception within the public, which would serve the interests of the establishment, the government and its policies? Each of these questions, in its turn, poses a serious theoretical challenge which the critical literature sometimes ignores. In this chapter, I would like to take up the first question, and offer a different approach to the issue of *falsehood*, a different approach, that is, to the understanding of what is wrong with media representations which seem to be *biased*.

The question of truth vs. falsehood, as originally formulated, cannot avoid the delicate and complex issue of *objective reality*. In a slightly outdated jargon, the demand for accurate reporting uses this very word – it calls for "objective" reporting. This demand presupposes a single, "objective" description of reality – and critically analyzes the coverage in terms of its *fit* with this description. In the context of the Israeli–Palestinian conflict, most of the critical (and all of the radical) literature presupposes an "objective" description of reality which centers around the occupation, the historical background of colonialism, the refugee problem and the systematic violations of human rights in the territories. Comparing the type of coverage exemplified in the Introduction with such a description obviously renders the coverage outrageously false, but the philosophical foundation of this comparison is shaky, to say the least: it seems almost redundant to explicate this after the post-structuralist revolution, but the above description of reality is itself a conceptual frame, a narrative, a symbolic representation. It is formulated from a certain point of view; it is based on a certain conception of history, a certain ideology. The description may thus provide a solid foundation for moral criticism and political activism – just like any other well-founded ideological system – but it can hardly function as a standard against which to assess the *factual* accuracy of news reports.[1]

This, then, is the first horn of a familiar dilemma: the naive notion of "objective" reality – and, by implication, the naive notion of truth – can no longer play a viable role in our interpretation of social texts. The other horn of the dilemma is the unfortunate fact that this very insight has all too often deteriorated in the public debate (and often enough in the academic literature) into an uncritical, amoral acceptance of all social texts as valid representations of one point of view or the other – seemingly leaving us with no foundation whatsoever for critical reasoning. To be sure, the fact that epistemic relativism potentially implies moral indifference lies at the very heart of the insistence, in radical circles, on the old notion of objective truth, but this, quite obviously, amounts to ignoring the problem rather than trying to solve it. The question, then, is this: can a theoretically valid solution to this problem be found, which, on the one hand, accepts the inevitable understanding that objective truth can no longer play a role in critical discourse, and, on the other hand, allows for morally relevant judgments of bias in the construction of the news? Such a solution, I believe, is indeed possible.

Accepting the idea that no objective description of reality can be found allows us to reconnect critical discourse to three simple observations about the *production* of news (and, by implication, with the relevant technical changes, to the production of social texts in general). The first is this: news producers have no better access to objective reality than do critical researchers. Senior editors are sometimes "in the know" about some things that they do not publish (because of either state or self-imposed censorship[2]), but this does not mean they are any closer to the type of knowledge one could call *objective*. There simply is no such thing.

The second empirical observation is that systematic patterns of ideological bias in the news are always the result of *editorial policy*. The policy need not be formally explicated. Most of the time, it is implicitly reformulated on every working day at the news desk, as the accumulative result of internal power struggles between different members of the editorial staff, in formal meetings and consultations and informal discussions. Editorial policy is determined through struggles about ideology, about power and control over management and production, about the interpretation of the events to be reported, about news value, the quality of sources, the interests of the paper as a business, the possible coverage strategies which the competing media may adopt, and, most importantly, about the expectations of the public. The policy, in other words, is the reflection of the editorial *habitus* at the news desk, that socially conditioned set of "lasting, transposable dispositions", in Bourdieu's famous words, which allow editors, at every given moment, to generate and organize their professional practices.[3] When the paper finally goes to print, the end product is the result of this policy.

But how can we talk about a policy of ideological bias if we do not accept objective reality as the basis for comparison? Well, this is where the third observation plays a crucial role: editorial policy asserts itself most clearly in editorial *work*. Think about the examples we have looked at in the Introduction: virtually everything we saw – the contradistinction "between the Hague and Jerusalem", the headlines addressing the judges in the Hague and the Israeli public, the formulation of all the other headlines, the decision to display Fanny Haim's letter and the photo of the wounded soldier all over the front page – these are the products of editorial work. In fact, we have not looked at the reports at all. In principle, the two newspapers could have decided to publish their February 23 editions *without the reports* – the headlines, images and graphic design would have sent the same emotional and ideological message with equal efficiency.

The notion of a newspaper without reports may sound absurd, but as the literature on news reading and comprehension shows quite clearly, this notion provides a pretty good first approximation of what news-consumers actually consume. Modern newspaper readers scan the paper, usually from front to back, look at the headlines and images, and only occasionally read the fine print. This is a perfectly rational mode of behavior, because newspaper headlines come with what might be thought of, in terms borrowed from Dan Sperber and Dierdre Wilson, a "guarantee" of *optimal relevance*:[4] they offer the readers the optimal ratio between *cognitive effect* (the amount of new and relevant information they provide) and *cognitive cost* (the effort it takes to read and interpret them). Simple considerations of cognitive cost-effectiveness, in an environment overflowing with information, thus dictate that most of the time, most people actually read headlines much more than they read reports. Moreover, when readers do read the reports themselves (or their first paragraphs), they read them *within the interpretative framework* constructed by the headlines. These headlines, coupled with the positioning of the piece in the paper, and the surrounding visual semiotics, provide the readers of newspapers with an *interpretative key*, the importance of which goes well beyond the specific pieces of information included in the reports. Exactly the same generalization applies to the editorial text in *television news broadcasts*: there, the interpretative key is communicated by the edition's headlines, the allocation of time slots for each report in the line-up, and the structure of the discourse in the studio between anchors, reporters and commentators – not just in terms of what they say, but also, and sometimes importantly, in terms of their body language and facial expressions. The interpretative key, as we shall see, not only provides a set of rules of interpretation for the specific news of the day, it actually, and much more significantly, provides a set of *identity markers* – it tells readers something of importance about *themselves*.

How, then, does all this help us rethink the notion of bias? Well, let us think of editors and reporters as producing two very different *types* of text, performing, in other words, two very different types of speech acts. Reporters produce a certain type of text *for their editors*, that is, an accumulation of pieces of information gathered from the field and accepted from sources. Editors receive this text as input, and produce a very different type of text – one which addresses the *readers*. Let us, then, leave the question of objective reality behind, and concentrate our critical analysis on the *intertextual* relationship between these different layers of text. Let us think of the reports and the commentaries – everything that eventually appears as small print in the paper – as the best *first approximation to reality* which the newspaper, the entire enterprise, managed to get hold of on a certain day. Then, let us reformulate the question of bias in the following manner: to what extent does the editorial text provide a fair reflection of the first approximation to reality provided by the reporters? In other words, to what extent did the newspaper editors actually follow the reports handed to them by their own reporters in their construction of the interpretative key for their readers?

It might be argued that the notion of the *best first approximation to reality* is an attempt to bring objective reality back into the picture, so to speak, through the back door: if some description of reality may count as a good first approximation to reality, then the distinction between this description and the real thing, that description of reality which is *really* objective, may seem to be a matter of degree, not of essence. This is definitely not what I intend the notion of "a first approximation" to mean. What matters to me is the fact that, whereas editors, both in newspapers and on TV, only have access to *descriptions of reality*, reporters have some access to reality itself, in the sense that, if they do their work correctly, they experience things on the ground. As different reporters experience different aspects of the way things are, their reports do *not* accumulate into a coherent, clear-cut description. It is exactly because of this, because the different reports tell different stories, that we can think of all of them *together* as a first-approximation to reality, and it is because of this that the comparison with the editorial text – which is coherent and clear-cut – is so important. Obviously, nothing guarantees that the reports are *valid*. Some of them, as we shall see, are direct reflections of government propaganda. The important thing, however, is that all of the reports, taken together – including all the ways in which they contradict each other – produce a complexity which, as a first approximation, reflects more of the complexity of reality than the editorial text.

Going back to the two newspapers we looked at in the Introduction, then, we quite obviously find that *some* of the reports reflect the same attitude we saw in the headlines. Here, for example, is reporter Sefi Hendler's attempt to put the ICJ trial in historical context:

Today, at 10 a.m. precisely, the clerk at the Hague international court will rise and announce: "The case of the advisory evaluation committee regarding the legal ramifications of the wall built in the occupied Palestinian territories." Fifteen solemn judges, clad in black gowns and white neck-cloths, will march into the courtroom. They will invite hundreds of spectators to take their seats – and the wall trial will commence.

True – this is only an advisory evaluation, not an enforceable resolution. And yet, it will be the realization of the dream cherished by the Arab states for years. Israel, the Jewish state, is to be judged, literally, by the world at large. For the first time in the international court's history, the trial will be broadcast live on television as well as the Internet. Citizens of the world will be able to surf to the court's website and look at the line of prosecutors who will rise to expose Israel's disgrace to the entire world. By the way, this is the first time the court has submitted to these wonders of modern technology, and it is hard to avoid the suspicion that this fossilized institution wishes to use the world's most popular conflict in order to regain its youth.

The fact of the matter, however, is that this is far from being typical. Much of the material that never appears at the level of editorial text *does* appear in the reports – but is systematically published (by the editors) *without* the appropriate headlines, usually on back pages. Thus, for example, the report published by *Ma'ariv* on page 8 quotes a manifesto distributed in the territories, according to which the attack in Jerusalem is "a reaction to the construction of the wall". This is not mentioned in the page's headline. In the commentary on the same page, reporter Amit Cohen writes:

> In any case, [the Palestinians] say, our problems will not be solved by the international court. Even the highly refined Palestinian diplomacy, which arouses envy in Israel, does not really impress the Palestinians themselves. Why, at the very same time their official spokesmen display their fluent English, bulldozers continue to build the fence. As far as they are concerned, this effort is meaningless, and has not succeeded in relieving, even slightly, the closures inflicted upon them.

On page 5 of the same edition appears a commentary by senior reporter Avraham Tirosh, under the headline: "Two Charred Chassis". The rest of the page is covered by a horrifying picture of a school textbook, drenched in blood, that belonged to one of the pupils killed in the attack in Jerusalem. Nothing in the page indicates that the commentary itself is actually highly critical of the wall:

> All in all, this fence has entangled Israel in a serious complication. It was not erected in time, and by the time it was erected, due to the pressure of the lethal reality, and after Sharon, Mofaz and others were good enough to change their minds, political reasons dictated the invention of a serpentine and illogical route, a sure and predictable recipe for trouble. This route has turned the fence, conceived as a wall to defend Israelis from those who do not wish them well, into a humanitarian hazard for innocent Palestinian civilians. It has separated them from their lands, played into the hands of all those who opposed the fence, and has led us to the Hague.

And on page 15 of *Yediot Ahronot*, far away from the "hard news" pages, alongside a story about safety seats for toddlers, appears a report about a speech given by Brigadier General Elazar Stern, the commander of the IDF education force, the officer personally responsible for maintaining and developing the IDF's ethical code:

> At a youth convention, yesterday, Brig. Gen. Stern said that the importance of the IDF's soldiers' values has changed during the Intifada, and we now allow ourselves actions we hadn't permitted when the confrontation began. "The soldiers' moral criteria have changed according to reality on the ground and level of risk to the soldiers", he said. "When I maintain the purity of my military ethical code, I make great connection with my pillow: I sleep wonderfully. But another eight people killed at the bombing today will never again see their pillow at night." Brig. Gen. Stern explained that the IDF is not interested in harming the innocent, and does not do so, but "this reality has been imposed on us".

This is a clear and robust phenomenon: a close reading of the entire set of reports sent in by the newspapers' correspondents reveals a complexity which is in no way reflected in the clear-cut, black-and-white, emotionally laden picture drawn by the editorial text. As we shall see, the fact that the stories which do not get mentioned in the editorial text nevertheless do get published in small print plays a crucial role in the construction of the interpretative key: publishing stories of this type in the back pages, or entirely without headlines, does something that simply *censoring* them would never be able to do. The fact that Brig. Gen. Stern's words, for example, appear in the back pages of the paper, so far away from the pages dedicated to Intifada coverage, sends a message to the readers which is far more significant than the story itself. It says that Stern's perspective, in fact the entire issue of the IDF's ethical standards in its operations in the territories, is *thematically unrelated* to any of the questions which are at the top of the Israeli agenda within the Israeli perspective. Most importantly, it is thematically unrelated to the question of *guilt*, which lies at the center of the contradistinction between the ICJ hearings and the reality of terror. Moreoever, the fact that internal criticism of the wall, or the Palestinian conviction that no diplomatic effort will reduce their suffering, are not reflected in any way in the editorial text, tells the readers who *do* get to the fine print that the newspaper – as an interpretative authority – is well aware of these complicating elements, that it has taken them into account, and has decided that they should not be taken seriously.

As I show in my book *Intifada Hits the Headlines*,[5] which analyzes the Israeli press coverage of the outbreak of the Intifada in October 2000, patterns of editorial bias of this type play a fundamental role in the construction of public opinion. Thus, to mention a single example, one of the most important questions the media had to deal with in October 2000 was Yasser Arafat's personal responsibility for the outbreak of the Intifada. Reporters received relevant information from about ten different sources about this question. As it turned out, nine of the ten insisted that the riots were a spontaneous outburst of Palestinian anger and frustration, following the long stalemate in negotiations and Ariel Sharon's visit to the Temple Mount. These sources included not only Palestinian and American officials, but also, importantly, senior sources in the IDF, the Israeli Secret Service (*Shin-Bet*) and the Israeli police. A single source repeatedly declared that Arafat planned and initiated the Intifada: Prime Minister Ehud Barak. Crucially, the editorial text of all major newspapers concentrated on Barak's contention, which captured all the major headlines, and was framed in them as a *factual* statement. All the statements of the other sources were published by the papers, but systematically in back pages, weekly supplements and so on, most of the time with no headlines. Thus, the majority view gleaned from the sources never managed to enter public discourse, whereas Barak's statement became the cornerstone of the new consensual perception, that is, the notion that Barak did everything possible to achieve a final-status agreement with the Palestinian Authority, only to see his "generous offers" flatly rejected in Camp David by Arafat, who then "proved" that his regime was not "ready for peace" by initiating the Intifada. This perspective, as we shall see in this book, was still the most crucial determinant of the interpretative frame proposed by the Israeli media 18 months later – long into Ariel Sharon's term in office.

The essence of bias, then, is *not* about *knowledge* vs. *ignorance*, *truth* vs. *falsity*, or *publication* vs. *censorship*, but about the investment of pieces of information with different types of *significance* – and, again, not just in terms of their significance as news, but also, and importantly so, in terms of their significance for the construction of social identity. This perspective, I will argue, not only allows for an analysis of bias which rests on a sound basis, both philosophically and empirically. As I will show in Chapter 6, it also provides a key to an understanding of the overall function of bias – an understanding which the objectivist perspective fails to grasp.

3
Commitment, Despair and Confusion: The Newspapers

The following two chapters describe the overall perspectives offered by the editorial texts of the five media during operation Defensive Shield. This chapter focuses on the printed press.

MA'ARIV: "THE PRICE WE PAY FOR OUR MORALITY"

Throughout operation Defensive Shield, *Ma'ariv* functions as a partisan newspaper in the simplest sense of the word, conveying a fascinating, fundamentalist version of dogmatic and belligerent Zionism. In this sense, it is the easiest to decipher. At a certain point, the paper actually revives the usage of this very term, Zionism, a word which for a long time has seldom been used with positive connotations by Hebrew speakers. On Independence Day, April 16, for example, *Ma'ariv* publishes a special supplement titled "And Yet ... ". "We concede," writes chief editor Amnon Dankner in the introduction to the supplement, "that this is a Zionist supplement, if you pardon the term, patriotic – God forbid – and optimistic. Yes, strange though this may seem, optimistic during these very days. We have already been to those horrible movies in black-and-white, and we are still hanging on, and shall continue doing so." *Ma'ariv* explicitly sends its readers a clear message: the Palestinians have declared war, we must fight for our very existence, and we should do it with *pride*. From this, everything else follows: there is absolutely no difference between the "infrastructure of terrorism" and the Palestinian Authority, and there can be no doubts with respect to the IDF's ability to "demolish the ritual of death" (these are the words chosen by chief editor Dankner for the title of his April 1, 2002 article). And the paper blatantly, defiantly, fends off guilt in every way possible. It takes no interest whatsoever in the Palestinians – they might indeed be suffering, but if so, they have only themselves to blame – and it is genuinely infuriated with the parliamentary opposition. As long as IDF soldiers are "fighting to protect our homes", the paper will not assist the opposition in its efforts to undermine the nation's endurance.

This pugnacious stance is encountered on each page, in each headline, and it trickles down to almost every commentary. The March 29 main headline, which appeared two days after the terror attack on Netanya's Park Hotel, has become famous worldwide:

With A Strong Hand and With An Outstretched Arm

This is a direct quotation from the Hagada, the traditional text read aloud during the Seder, the Passover ceremony. In the original text, God saved the children of Israel from slavery in Egypt "with a strong hand and with an outstretched arm, with great terror and with signs and wonders". In the paper, the powerful phrase becomes an explicit call for tough military action. The headline on page 3, another quotation from the Hagada, spread over a huge photograph of the large pool of blood on the Park Hotel's floor, contextualizes the terror attack in the persecution-ridden history of the Jewish people:

In Every Generation They Have Risen Against Us to Annihilate Us

These headlines are all the more significant because *Ma'ariv* is an avowedly *secular* newspaper. Quotations from religious text do not regularly find their way onto the paper's pages. *Ma'ariv* thus tells its readers something about *identity*: today, secular or religious, we are all *Jews*.

Interestingly, these headlines stirred some controversy within the journalistic community in Israel, and Nahum Barnea expressed the views of many others when he wrote in the journalists' monthly *The Seventh Eye*, that in the first days of the operation there were some people in the media "who acted like fools ... like [those who formulated] *Ma'ariv*'s main headline when the action started". This remark is as important as the headline itself, because Barnea's critical stance reflects a defense strategy we shall encounter throughout this book: it shrugs off the headline as folly, and completely refrains from a more extensive political, social and psychological discussion of the conditions which made this "folly" possible. Barnea is well aware that headlines such as this – outrageous, overly creative, silly – are suggested daily at editorial meetings. This is an endless source of amusement for the editors, but at the end of the day, in more regular times, such headlines do not get printed. As we shall see, Barnea's evasion exemplifies one of the ways the Israeli media suppresses guilt: when IDF activity results in the death of a Palestinian child, it is always framed as a *mistake*, just as looting and vandalism perpetrated by IDF soldiers are always *exceptions*.

Three articles are published on *Ma'ariv's* front page on March 29, under a large picture of the blood on the hotel's floor. The authors are former Prime Minister Binyamin Netanyahu, leading journalist Dan Margalit, and chief editor Dankner. Together, they express the paper's stand in no uncertain terms. "Since that Yom Kippur (in 1973) until this Passover", writes Netanyahu,

> we have not experienced such rampant Arab violence accompanied by such profound disdain for our nation and our heritage. The Palestinian terrorists are telling us: we will murder you whenever the opportunity arises ... This is the principal and true aim of Arafat's terror regime – not to establish a state, but rather to destroy one ... We must do what any other normal nation would do under such circumstances: stop the in-fighting, respond with war and repress the enemy who threatens our very existence.

Margalit is a shade more subdued:

> As the parliamentary debate approached, there was a great increase in the number of ministers in favour of military action more powerful than any the region has known since Arafat initiated this Intifada ... The government is entering a new phase in its battle against Palestinian terrorism, and it does so with the support of the vast majority of the Israeli public.

Dankner, for his part, does not mince words. Here is just one paragraph from his article:

> It's time to set things straight, time to repair Israel's deterrent power. We are a tremendously powerful nation, almost daily put to shame by weak enemies who attack it, while it refrains from showing its true force in response, deterrence and prevention ... There comes a time when a nation must turn its back on petty internal squabbles and unite in order to fight for its very

life. Before we resume the debates about whether or not we should accept the Saudi initiative, about the pros and cons of the separation fence, about withdrawal or retrenchment in the territories, we must all come together to protect our very souls, to protect our lives, which have become so totally impossible.

Toward the end of the article, Dankner declares that in such distressful days the media must also adopt a certain position:

We, the media, must also seriously consider what we are doing. We must ask ourselves whether, under the guise of arguments about the public's right to know and the press's right to go wherever it wants in order to expose no matter what, we are actually presenting as facts what is really the political approach favored by most journalists and editors. And in doing so, are we not weakening the spirit and undermining the power of all echelons of the political and military establishments, down to the lowest-ranking fighters in the field? Should we not learn a lesson from the press in great democracies like the United States and Britain? They know how to cheer the public when weakness is impermissible, to support when it would be fatal to let go. Of course, in times like this the press should not spill boiling blood, sow hatred and push things to the limit. But we can demand decisive and comprehensive action in order to defend our lives. And we can join hands in encouraging those who have to make the decisions as well as those who will have to carry them out.

Where exactly runs the dividing line between a press that knows "how to support when it would be fatal to let go" and a press that "spill[s] boiling blood, sow[s] hatred and push[es] things to the limit"? Dankner clearly crosses this tenuous line in his front-page article of April 1, when he writes: "The Arabs' dismal ritual of death does not discriminate between peaceniks and settlers, between hawks and doves, between extremists and moderates. And so, all of these should now unite in order to fight this malignant ritual, to overpower it, crush it, demolish it." But this is not the most important point. The really important issue is that *Ma'ariv* adopts a formal policy in these lines, a policy which has very little to do with the coverage of the operation itself – its development, its goals, its possible results – and everything to do with "cheering the public when weakness is impermissible". *Ma'ariv*'s policy, quite simply, is exactly that of an active participant in the operation. The fact that this is *not* the case in the other media, as we shall see later on, will play an important role in the attempt, to be taken up in Chapter 6, to rethink the common denominator of all the different perspectives of the Israeli media in terms of identity, rather than in terms of the manufacture of consent.

In line with its policy, *Ma'ariv* goes out of its way to prove that the general public entirely supports operation Defensive Shield. Morale-boosting items popular in the 1950s now appear in the paper almost daily, featuring totally committed reserve soldiers reporting at their units. The leading article in the April 4 daily supplement, for instance, carries a report about Sharon's visit to a reserve unit in the occupied territories. The item is replete with jubilant statements about the reserve soldiers' unwavering commitment. In reporter Eli Kamir's words, they "have no doubts". The supplement is headed: "A Warm Welcome". The article itself, on pages 2–3, is titled: "We Didn't Ask Why, We Just Came". The story's subtitles, teasers and picture caption are all dedicated to the same goal. Each of them addresses a possible doubt – and immediately sets things straight: There is no political debate, no moral constraints, no personal problems, no financial hardships, no conscientious objectors. Everyone is joining hands "to get the job done". Here are some of the teasers:

> The Prime Minister got a real boost during a visit at an army base on the demarcation line, the day before yesterday. He was received by a group of reservists from the right and from the left – all of whom had recently received their summons and reported to the base. "I don't want to sound pompous," said one of the officers, "but the people here are ready to sacrifice everything, even their lives. We put aside all our personal problems, and came here to get the job done."

> The Prime Minister wanted to know what the reservists were doing in their civilian lives, how their businesses were doing, what they felt. "Our work is affected," said one of them, "but we'll handle it."

Sharon left the meeting and ran to the helicopter, which was all wet from the rain. He touched the seats, found a relatively dry one and sat down. Then he took a candy bar out of his pocket, gave it to a woman sitting on his left and smiled all the way home to his farm

Lieutenant-Colonel A.: "I have no moral qualms. I have only one moral obligation – towards my kids and my home. My only commitment in this war is to them."

The reservists [tell] Sharon: "Conscientious objection is a marginal phenomenon. We, here, are giving the answer on the ground – by our very numbers."

Could this actually be a reasonable, factual report about a group of dedicated reserve soldiers who simply happen to have this set of beliefs? Yes, this is theoretically possible. But actually reserve soldiers have confronted Sharon with tough questions on visits of this type, and these confrontations, which are reported by the *other* media, are flatly ignored by *Ma'ariv*. Thus, for example, Sharon met with soldiers during his visit to Jenin on April 10, and *Yediot Ahronot* reported this encounter on page 3 of the next day's issue, under the headline:

Soldier to Sharon in Jenin: We May Continue Taking
Kids Out of their Homes, But What Next?

Ma'ariv, on the other hand, only presents its readers with a photograph of the meeting (a reminder that a picture may not always be worth a thousand words), with the following caption:

Sharon and Mofaz at army headquarters in the Jenin area, yesterday: "We will not budge till the job is done."

Within this context, *Ma'ariv* finds very little interest in the stories brought in by its own reporter Eli Kamir, about the slapdash decision-making process in the cabinet, and the disagreements between Sharon and Minister Shimon Peres regarding the entire operation. The behind-the-scenes report – which should mostly remind the Israeli reader how Sharon himself, as Minister of Defense, managed to persuade the government to invade Lebanon in 1981 – is buried on page 10 of the March 31 issue. None of this reaches any of the paper's headlines. A similar policy is adopted with respect to the political opposition: quotes from opposition leaders never reach the headlines, unless they are sufficiently provocative for readers to perceive them as treacherous. Such comments anger *Ma'ariv*, and it is precisely for this reason that they deserve to make headlines. This happens primarily with comments by Arab speakers, for example:

Mk Mahoul Raised his Arm in Nazi Salute at Knesset

A Sakhnin Newspaper: "Put Murderer Sharon Under Siege"

Mk Tibi: "The Resistance in Jenin is an Act of Noble Heroism"

Israeli Arabs in Shefar'am Say Prime Minister Should be Killed

Ironically, the Jewish political opposition is mentioned on *Ma'ariv*'s front page only once during the entire month. On April 22, right-wing writer Eyal Meged publishes an op-ed article, which was ceremoniously promoted to the front page. The article is titled "My Friends on the Left Make Me Feel Ashamed".

How, then, does *Ma'ariv* present operation Defensive Shield itself to its readers? What type of policy does it adopt with respect to the day-by-day coverage of the *news*? First, the paper readily accepts the Defense Minister's order to prevent Israeli and foreign reporters from entering the fighting zone. The restriction was announced on the day the operation began, and was only lifted after the first ten, decisive days. Throughout this period, all the Israeli media used materials they received from various IDF sources, materials that were mostly processed and mediated. As media critic Aviv Lavie wrote in *Ha'aretz* on April 2, this was one of the reasons for "the difference between what is reported and shown here, and what the rest of the world – especially the Arab world – hears and sees":

The Israeli media does not have real information about what is going on ... Since the journalists are not there to see things for themselves, the soldiers become their sources ... On the Arab TV stations (but not only there) we could see IDF soldiers taking over hospitals, damaging medical equipment and medicine, locking up doctors and keeping them away from their patients ... The entire world sees injured Palestinians bleeding on the streets, and hears accounts about the IDF stopping ambulances on their way to treat them. The entire world hears Palestinian citizens saying that they cannot leave their homes because "the soldiers shoot everyone on the street." The entire world hears reports about Palestinian families under siege in their homes for three days and nights – without water or electricity, and in some cases with dwindling food supplies. There are also stories about plunder and looting. These might all be propagandist lies (though in some of the cases, the photographs speak for themselves), but Israeli journalists have no way of getting at the truth, so as to deny the claims or confirm them. Given this inability, our television studios endlessly circulate the same slogans – to the effect that "we have no issue with the civilian population" – and reports about the amazing care with which IDF soldiers go about their work.[1]

Ma'ariv is not troubled by all that, and it does not even try to fight for its autonomy. Its editorials do not mention that the area has been closed to the press, its front pages do not carry items about the topic, and the reports are formulated as if written by correspondents in the field. Reading the paper, one may not even guess that its reporters' work is restricted in any way.

But there is more: when it must decide between its identity as a newspaper and its identity as an *Israeli* newspaper, *Ma'ariv*'s position is clear-cut. Throughout the operation, it publishes a long list of complaints about the foreign media's anti-Israeli bias. On April 2, for example, it prints two photographs, side by side: Under the caption "The picture that got published", appears a photo of an IDF soldier confronting a television crew. Under the caption "The picture that did not get published", appears a photo of a Palestinian accused of collaborating with Israel, who was lynched by a local mob. *Ma'ariv* – on behalf of all Israelis – is offended by the discriminatory attitude of the world media. This sense of injury conveys a deep message: it portrays the foreign media as engaging in a *discourse of blame* against Israel. Toward the end of the operation, *Ha'aretz* is also added to the *Ma'ariv*'s blacklist: on April 28, the newspaper opens its daily supplement with a letter from writer-celebrity Irit Linor, happy to announce that she is cancelling her subscription to *Ha'aretz* because it makes her "feel ashamed of her Zionism". The supplement is titled: "Left the Country", a pun on the name of the blacklisted paper: "Ha'aretz" literally means "the country".[2]

Significantly, *Ma'ariv's* position regarding the closure of the area to the Israeli press is not identical to that of its own military correspondent, Yoav Limor. Limor's attitude is fascinating: he is truly worried about the press's independence, but he also regards the decision as a tactical error on the part of the senior military ranks, a mistake that seriously harms the Israeli image. He writes of IDF officers and soldiers on the ground, who would have liked to see the Israeli correspondents there – in order to be able to present their own point of view. On April 9, in a small item published at the bottom of page 7, Limor writes that "senior army officials are severely critical of the army commanders' and political echelon's decision not to allow coverage of the war in the occupied territories". The following paragraph makes it crystal clear that what the army officials are worried about is nothing but the issue of guilt:

"They make us look like war criminals. But anyone who would see footage from the ground would know that the opposite is the case," said an officer serving in the Nablus kasbah .... It appears that the policy of a media black-out not only aroused the anger of the media in Israel and abroad, but also created an uproar within the IDF itself. Contrary to senior army officials' claims that "the commanders on the ground do not want reporters in their way in the midst of battle," it seems that the officers would actually like their activity to be seen in the Israeli media, and even more so in the international media. They believe that Israel is abandoning the field to the Palestinians, who "broadcast tendentious pictures, very remote from reality".

And so, *Ma'ariv* continuously presents its readers with an unambiguously "positive" coverage of the events: the IDF is engaged in a life-and-death battle against the very roots of Palestinian terrorism. The IDF captures terrorists who appear on its "wanted" lists; it kills "armed" terrorists; it uncovers explosives factories, and, of course, it accumulates *incriminating evidence* against Yasser Arafat, who is sitting all the while in his *muqata'a*, totally surrounded by Israeli tanks. And all the while, the IDF is doing everything possible to help the Palestinian civilian population make it peacefully through the events. This is the story narrated by hundreds of headlines throughout the month. The headlines which might be interpreted as hinting at greater complexity can be counted on one hand. Here is a representative sample of the "operational" headlines:

Captured in Battle: Equipment for Tapping IDF Communications

Hundreds of Thousands of Forged Israeli Shekels
Found at Arafat's Muqata'a in Ramallah

Idf: We Have Proven the Link Between Arafat and Terror

IDF Reveals: Arafat Approved Financing for Terror

Reservist Soldier was Recruited Last Week, Killed by Sniper Fire

"There's a Terrorist or a Bomb Hiding in Every Hole"

"The Roads Exploded Under Our Feet"

The End of the Passover-Massacre Mastermind

"It took us Two Days of Heavy Fighting
to Advance Only 450 Meters"

The visual materials accompanying the texts are of the same nature: never-ending convoys of armored vehicles; dusty, smiling soldiers with tired, unshaven faces, and countless displays of seized arms.

And where are the Palestinian citizens? What is happening to *them* in the meantime? Well, during this month, half of the headlines published by *Ma'ariv* which have anything to do with the Palestinian population highlight generous humanitarian gestures by Israeli soldiers, physicians and civilians. Some of these are quite remarkable:

Terror Victim's Family will meet Arab Woman
who Received his Kidney Donation

Soldiers Evacuated House in Bethlehem – Gave Family 1500 Shekels

Soldiers Clean Arafat's Bethlehem Palace

IDF Sources: We Conveyed Humanitarian Aid to Jenin

Army Doctor Delivered Baby of Jerusalem Suicide-Bomber's Relative

What else does *Ma'ariv* offer its readers? Well, another five headlines cover "deviant" behavior, that is, individual soldiers and civilians who are suspected of having acted in unacceptable ways and will be appropriately prosecuted:

"Jewish Underground" Suspected of Killing a Palestinian Yesterday

IDF Investigates Reports about Soldiers Engaged
in Plunder and Looting

Reservist Accused of Shooting and Wounding a Palestinian Woman

First Soldier Detained for Looting While Conducting Searches
in the Territories

First Charges Brought for Looting During Operation
Defensive Shield

One headline deals with Palestinian children: "Palestinian Boy Carrying a Bag Full of Explosives Arrested in Jenin". One huge headline is dedicated to the Palestinian health system: "Explosive Belt Found in Palestinian Ambulance". Another headline touches on the living conditions in the Jenin refugee camp: "'Only the Martyrs' Families are Doing Well'". And, finally, three small headlines contrast what the *others* are saying about the situation in the territories with what Israel's legal system has to say about it:

Physicians for Human Rights: "Conditions in Territories
Near Catastrophe"

Court Appeal: Prison Conditions are "Sub-human"

Supreme Court: IDF Does Not Infringe Humanitarian Guidelines
in the Territories

Where are the dead and the injured? The curfew that lasted for weeks? The water and food shortages? The bulldozers? The destruction of civilian infrastructure? The parceling of the West Bank into isolated cantons? The thousands of civilians who lost their homes? The thousands detained? None of these appear in

Ma'ariv. The headlines, separately and together, reflect nothing but a desperate attempt to fend off guilt: they insist that Israel "does not infringe humanitarian guidelines in the territories"; that those violations of human rights that do occur are always *exceptional* cases, performed by *individuals*, who are to be punished by the state; that the other side is the one to blame for using *children* and *ambulances* in the service of terror. Finally, the headlines assert that even the day-to-day reality in the refugee camps is the Palestinians' own responsibility, and that only those who engage in terror manage to make a living.

This attitude is most starkly revealed following the Palestinian claims about a "massacre" in Jenin. Before we examine *Ma'ariv*'s coverage of this issue, however, some general remarks about the events in the Jenin refugee camp and their coverage are required. Reports from within the refugee camp – both in the Israeli and the international media – were quickly overshadowed by the Palestinian accusations about a planned IDF massacre. Such a massacre did not take place. As media critic Aviv Lavie wrote in his *Ha'aretz* column on April 26, these Palestinian claims resulted in part from a decision to exploit the uncertainty about events in the camp for short-term propaganda purposes, but they were also partly the result of real hysteria: "When the battle smoke was densest," said one Palestinian journalist to Lavie, "people outside the camp were frustrated, feeling that something terrible was happening inside." When it finally emerged that no such massacre had occurred, Israel gained a few significant points in the propaganda war: it now had "evidence" of the overall falsity of Palestinian reports. Needless to say, the entire Israeli media immediately rejected the massacre accusations. But this fact by no means exhausts the discussion about the way they covered the Jenin events. The significant point is that they concentrated, almost without exception, on the accusations themselves, on the very fact that Israel was being accused – even after it became clear that other Palestinian claims, severe in their own right, were much more accurate than those concerning a possible massacre.

When Jenin hits the headlines, then, *Ma'ariv* fully enlists in the defense of the soldiers who participated in the events there, presenting the Jenin affair as the most glaring evidence for the soldiers' *innocence*. The paper explicitly represents their perspective, and lashes out against any argument brought against them by the Palestinians, by foreign sources, and also, most importantly, by Israeli army and government sources who expressed their doubts about sending reserve soldiers on such a difficult mission. In this case, then, *Ma'ariv* chooses to concentrate on the suppression of guilt as an identity issue – *we* are not guilty – at the expense of supporting the IDF as part of the establishment.

During the first few days of the Jenin battle, the paper publishes detailed daily reports of the hardships endured by the troops fighting in the refugee camp (again, it should be remembered, the paper has no correspondents there). The Palestinian perspective is totally absent. The paper's daily supplement on April 8, for example, publishes a report "from the field", under the headline "Explosive Devices in Every Home, Car and Pushcart". The long subheadline elaborates:

> The subjugation of Jenin refugee camp has become the hardest and most bloody task so far, because the Palestinians prepared themselves for the IDF invasion in every possible way. Fighters were met with hundreds of explosive devices set off on every street-corner, in sewage holes, on trees and electricity poles and in windows. "We encountered explosives and shooting every step of the way," said an IDF soldier.

The next day, April 9, 13 IDF soldiers were killed in the refugee camp. *Ma'ariv* went into head-on confrontation mode. The paper's headline on April 10 reads: "Death Trap in Jenin". Over the headline appears a quote from one of the wounded soldiers: "We paid a high price for trying our best not to hurt civilians."

The paper's editorial for that day is headed "The Price We Pay for our Morality", and it offers, quite simply, the most explicit and conscious conceptualization of the entire Israeli struggle in terms of the global discourse of blame:

> We can now start thinking about the war that will follow this war – the media and information war, in which we can expect Israel to be internationally accused for its actions during operation Defensive Shield ... Before this begins, we should make it clear to the world and to ourselves, on the morning

after this battle in Jenin, drenched with our soldiers' blood, that the heavy losses we suffered yesterday were the painful price for our insistence on fighting ethically ... Today, with our hearts full of sorrow for those we lost, and our heads bowed over their graves, we may also feel pride in the IDF's moral standards. Today, we may refrain from examining our fresh wounds and engaging in a critical analysis of the incident ... Facing the waves of criticism to be expected from abroad – and from within Israel as well – the majority of Israelis may hold their heads up high and say that we shall go on resisting by force whoever tries to sow destruction and terror among us.

From April 10 until the end of the operation, most of what appears in *Ma'ariv* – headlines, texts, commentaries – is mobilized to advance this perspective; heroic stories highlighting the dear price paid for the soldiers' high moral standards in Jenin are published on a daily basis. On April 11, for example, the front page of the daily supplement is titled "The Way, The Victims", with the following subtitle:

A father who lost his son in Jenin the day before yesterday spoke furiously while standing by the fresh grave: "The army sends soldiers to their death instead of bombing the place with aircraft", thus raising the question to what extent the IDF risks its soldiers' lives in order to protect the civilian population.

The article itself appears on pages 2 and 3 of the supplement, under the headline "The Dilemma", which is formulated in the subtitle: "Should we send soldiers into the alleys or use aircraft shelling, thus risking civilians? This is the question facing the IDF leadership."

On April 14, *Ma'ariv* publishes a first report from within the refugee camp, by military correspondent Yoav Limor. Limor was probably the first journalist to enter the camp. Interestingly, this was the outcome of a behind-the-scenes struggle between *Yediot Ahronot* and *Ma'ariv*: the former was given permission to publish an exclusive, festive feature from Arafat's *muqata'a*. *Ma'ariv*'s editor, Amnon Dankner, protested to the Chief of Staff and demanded an "equivalent". Limor walked about under military protection, and spoke with the soldiers, not with the Palestinians. Among other things, he wrote that "the devastation in the camp is tremendous. It is hard to describe. Battle was engaged for almost every house. Those walls that remain standing show marks of explosives and bullets. Some are covered with the soot resulting from helicopter shelling. Many houses simply have no walls: the bulldozers crushed them." The newspaper's headline and subheadline for the article, which are published on the front page, are a masterpiece of denial:

Special: Jenin – View From Within
Jihad-land

After the tough battle: havoc and stench. "This is the price of war", say the reservists, "they may be miserable, but it is their fault." The pictures of shaheeds [martyrs] hang on the walls. International media gives prominence to Palestinian claims about a "massacre" in Jenin.

All the guilt-oriented framing strategies discussed so far appear in this formulation: the upper headline, which promises a "view from within" – following a visit prearranged with the IDF; the headline which defines the entire place as "Jihad-land", and all its residents as terrorists; the subheadline which frames the devastation and foul odours as unfortunate yet unavoidable results of a "tough battle"; the reservists who readily acknowledge that the Palestinians "may be miserable", but immediately add that "it is their fault"; the "pictures of shaheeds" which "hang on the walls", as silent proof that the place is, indeed, "Jihad-land"; and beyond all this the fact that after all these examples of Palestinian treachery and IDF restraint, the world at large is quick to rally against Israel, and accept the Palestinian claims of a massacre. This headline is probably the most dramatic example we have seen, but one teaser, which appeared in the weekend supplement, offers serious competition: the article is headed "Things We Have Proven in Jenin". In the story, *Ma'ariv*'s former chief editor Yaakov Erez interviews (Reserve) Colonel Didi Yedidia, commander of the division which fought in Jenin. The editors of the supplement decided to highlight this quote from the colonel:

I really want to contradict a claim that has been hovering in the air. Our aggression, as the attacking party, was carried out on a linear slope. We did not start out with aggression and maintain a straight line. As resistance against us grew, so our aggression increased. The same is true for the helicopter gunships and other forces.

Here we find the serious, rational tone of a scientist, who finds it imperative "to contradict a claim that has been hovering in the air" about Israeli aggression in the camp. The colonel is genuinely trying to explain: as far as he was concerned, there was no need for all this aggression – it was forced on the soldiers by the *other* side. This clearheaded tone, devoid of demagoguery, which considers the conquest of a Palestinian refugee camp in terms of a mathematical formula, in which the IDF is always the innocent party, epitomizes the frightening rigidity of a mindset totally dedicated to the suppression of guilt – a mindset which dominated *Ma'ariv*'s coverage of the entire operation.

YEDIOT AHRONOT: "ON A SLIPPERY SLOPE LEADING TO WAR"

In direct opposition to *Ma'ariv*'s euphoric tone, *Yediot Ahronot*'s coverage of operation Defensive Shield reflects a deep sense of *despair*. More than anything else, the paper is fed up: it is fed up with the overall situation, with the wave of terror attacks, and with a government that, as far as the paper is concerned, does not know what it is doing. All this does not amount to a revisionistic view of the conflict: like *Ma'ariv*, *Yediot Ahronot* entirely accepts the fundamental notion that the only real culprit in this tragic story is Yasser Arafat. Like *Ma'ariv*, it expresses support for the reserve soldiers, takes no interest in the Palestinians, and is outraged, insulted, by the international accusations about the events in Jenin. But it does not share *Ma'ariv*'s indignant, belligerent attitude – despair has a moderating effect on the newspaper's general tone, which is more reserved. *Yediot Ahronot*'s approach is more pragmatic: its headlines are calmer, it allows for more exposure to the political opposition, publicly protests against the closure of the area to reporters, and dedicates extensive space to the reports of Tsadok Yekhezkeli, the one Israeli reporter who insisted on conducting independent investigations inside the Jenin refugee camp despite the closure. At times, this complex attitude evolves into a truly critical approach – especially with respect to Prime

Minister Sharon. The paper frankly and bluntly criticizes him for what it sees as a senseless recourse to revenge. As we shall see, this critical stand, as impressive at it is, nevertheless shies away from tackling the all-important question of Sharon's *strategic goals*. It characterizes him as a prime minister who does not know what he is doing, and systematically suppresses indications that the goal of operation Defensive Shield is not simply revenge and not the fight against terrorism, but the reoccupation of the West Bank and the destruction of the Palestinian Authority. *Yediot Ahronot*, then, does not attempt to rally support for the operation, but it does engage, in an interestingly complex way, in the suppression of guilt.

On March 29, the newspaper's main headline announces: "War on Arafat". In this sense, *Yediot Ahronot* does not distinguish itself from *Ma'ariv*. But four out of five front-page commentaries – written by the paper's four senior journalists – convey a sense of desperate, almost hostile, disbelief towards Sharon and his policy. The support they express for the military campaign is, at best, nominal. Below are four passages, by Nahum Barnea, Alex Fishman, Sima Kadmon and Sever Plotsker:[3]

> We are on a slippery slope leading to war. A war with no name and no aim, a war with no marching songs, no glorious conquests, a war in which yesterday's friend becomes today's foe ... True, the government has not officially announced that it plans to topple the Palestinian Authority – but it will get there eventually. So we might as well pose the difficult questions right now: who will fill the leadership void in the territories? Who will take charge of the population? How will Israel deal with suicide bombers when Arafat is gone? Because they will not disappear – whether Arafat is here or not.

> This ominous feeling of a suffocating personal siege, of a panic-stricken public, of a country on the verge of the abyss, of a wavering government, of the whole-world-is-against-us – all this we have had ample opportunity to experience on the eve of the Six Day War. And much like then, Israel, today, is gearing itself up to conquer the cities of the West Bank, in order to stop the suffocation ... We are still eating the rotten fruits of that war, day and night, every day. What fruits will the current

military exploit harvest? And what will the day after bring with it?

[The public's] faith in the country's power is not the same as hope – which has long been lost. Nor is it tantamount to trust in our leadership – there is none. We are left with Zinni's failed mission, the irrelevance of the Saudi plan, terror beyond the limits of our imagination, and the use of force, which provokes further terror, bringing more force, bringing more terror. This is the point we have reached: we refuse to disengage, to separate, and go on believing in the country's power. This is not faith. It is the sense of having no choice.

Israel's government repeatedly appeals to the revenge-retaliation weapon. Not because it is appropriate or effective, but because it is the only thing the ministers can agree on. As far as revenge is concerned, we do indeed have a national consensus ... Is this government in favor of toppling the Palestinian Authority or against it? In favor of the Saudi initiative or against it? In favor of expelling Arafat or against it? Depends on who you ask. The Foreign Minister says: this is not my government. The Prime Minister says: this is not my government ... It is a government best characterized by paralysis and stasis.

In line with this general sense of skepticism, the paper is more concerned than *Ma'ariv* with the government's decision-making process, and with the questions raised by senior members of the establishment with respect to the operation. Under the front-page headline of March 29 appears the following subtitle: "The plan: to conquer West Bank cities, topple the Palestinian authority, declare Arafat an 'enemy' and possibly deport him ... Labor may quit government".

A full double-spread, on pages 10 and 11, is dedicated to the decision-making process, under the logo – "What Does the Prime Minister Want?" The headlines and subheadlines emphasize the disagreements between Prime Minister Sharon, Minister Shimon Peres and Chief of Staff Shaul Mofaz:

Sharon's Plan: First – Isolation; Then – Deportation

Only One Minister Insisted: Deport Arafat

Only One Security Service Official in Favor of Deportation

Peres left the meeting worried, with a grim face. Said he was against the action "because no program was proposed, only an outline. This could be used to do things without approval, should anybody choose to do so."

Chief of Staff snubbed: told government that the operation's objective was "to change the security situation so as to enable political negotiations". Sharon furiously responded: "What are you talking about? There won't be any negotiation whatsoever."

Yediot Ahronot, then, is walking a fine line with respect to the question of the overall goals of the operation: it does not promote the issue to its front-page headlines, but it nevertheless dedicates ample space to the topic, and openly states, in its front-page commentaries and the entire double-spread, that the official goals of the operation leave too many questions unanswered. The comparison with *Ma'ariv*, which goes out of its way to supress the whole issue, is significant.

As far as the political opposition is concerned, *Yediot Ahronot*'s attitude is only slightly different from that of *Ma'ariv*. Generally, as in the rival paper, opposition Members of the Knesset (MKs) make headlines in *Yediot Ahronot* only when they say something outrageous – or strange enough for ridicule, for example:

MK Tibi Wept: "Arafat Will Die"

Violence During Leftists' Demo

MK Mahoul Saluted "Heil Sharon!" –
And Was Removed from the Knesset

But a few headlines do report the position of an opposition member in a straightforward manner (for example, "Member of Knesset Sarid to Sharon: Do Not Undo the Work of Begin and Rabin"). One headline even makes it to the front page on April 8: "Old-Time Labor Leader Yitzhak Ben Aharon: I Leave the Party". Under different circumstances, these sparse headlines would not be worth mentioning: *Yediot Ahronot* does not really offer the political opposition a serious and substantial platform, but its attitude is nevertheless a shade more tolerant than *Ma'ariv*'s. Things become much more interesting when we take a look at the way *Yediot Ahronot* deals with non-political, *grassroots* objections to the operation. Here, the paper proves that its editorial policy defies simple pigeon-holing. This is most dramatically demonstrated in what came to be known as the "Yafa Yarkoni affair".

At the age of 75, Yafa Yarkoni was the foremost singer-celebrity of the 1948 generation. She was known mainly as the "war troubadour": in all of Israel's wars, from 1948 onward, she would go to the front and sing to the soldiers (in the US, she was sometimes called "the Israeli Bob Hope"). Her songs and ballads are the backbone of Zionist popular music, the kind of songs broadcast every year on Memorial Day and Independence Day. In April 2002, a special concert was planned in her honor, with virtually all the celebrated musicians in Israel participating. But a week after the beginning of operation Defensive Shield, and 24 hours before Memorial Day, Yafa Yarkoni expressed her support for a group of conscientious objectors in a radio interview. "I think they are right", she said, "they have the right to follow their conscience." And, she added, "We are a people that went through the holocaust, how can we do these things?" The reaction was swift: the concert in her honor was cancelled.

Ma'ariv reacted predictably. On April 15, it dedicated a minuscule headline on page 14 to the event: "Yafa Yarkoni Supports Conscientious Objectors." The following day another headline announced: "Yafa Yarkoni's Concert Cancelled, Because of her Support for Conscientious Objectors". When Gidi Gov, a singer-celebrity of a younger generation, announced his decision to withdraw from the artists' union in protest at the concert's cancellation, the paper mentioned his action on page 18 of the April 23 issue, followed the next day by an op-ed article by chief editor Dankner, entitled: "She Deserves It". "Anyone who draws an analogy between the Palestinians and the Jews during the Holocaust, between the IDF and the Nazis," writes Dankner, "joins our most wicked enemies, and should be banned, condemned and disgraced." *Yediot Ahronot*, on the other hand, gave Yafa Yarkoni ample opportunity to explain her position, in an article published on April 13, entitled: "Yaffa Yarkoni: Pictures From Territories Resemble the Holocaust". Gidi Gov's withdrawal from the artists' union received a front-page headline, followed by an extensive feature in the inner pages, titled: "The War-Troubadour's War". Some weeks later, on May 3, the paper published a lengthy interview with the singer. The front-page headline, referring to the interview, simply said: "Yafa Yarkoni on Scapegoatism". *Ha'aretz*, by the way, entirely avoided the issue until the middle of May, and unlike *Yediot Ahronot* did not offer Yarkoni any defense.

All this is significant: when the international press voices some of the claims regarding Jenin, *Yediot Ahronot* carries an emotional editorial against the "moral lynching" of IDF soldiers. It also lashes out, explicitly and aggressively, against UN representative Terje Larssen, following his critical comments made while visiting the refugee camp. But in the "Yafa Yarkoni affair", the paper actually declares that it is in principle willing to listen to claims against Israel, as long as they come from within Israeli society, that is, as long as *we* – not the politicians, and definitely not the hostile world – criticize *ourselves*. The paper's attitude, then, is not directly about the IDF conduct in the territories, but about identity. Internal, grassroots criticism, for *Yediot Ahronot*, is not automatically associated with the discourse of blame.

This is why none of this contradicts the fact that *Yediot Ahronot* does its best to create a profound, almost religious, sense of identification with the soldiers in the field – regardless of the government's policy and the operation's objective. The paper publishes daily columns dedicated to the soldiers' lifestyle, reservists' complaints about the quality of army food, greetings to relatives and group photographs from the field – sometimes under the logo "To the Soldiers With Love". The headlines in these sections do their best to maximize the sense of solidarity expressed by the massive voluntary mobilization of reserve units:

"See You After the War"

"Happy Holidays, Put on Your Uniform"

"We are Very Worried, but we are Fighting for our Homes"

Captain Michal goes to War

The last headline, of course, is, again, all about identity: Captain Michal, a woman, "proves" that the sense of solidarity cuts across the barrier of gender.

As far as the unfolding action on the ground is concerned, *Yediot Ahronot* provides its readers with a fascinating combination. Until the events in Jenin, the paper tells the story from the army's viewpoint. The tone is less virulent than *Ma'ariv*'s, but the paper nevertheless does not take the Palestinian perspective into account. The headlines dealing with the Palestinian population are hardly worth mentioning: just like *Ma'ariv*, the paper publishes more headlines about Israeli generosity than about the Palestinian population's plight. Here are a few examples out of the hundreds of "action" headlines:

Terrorists on Every Street Corner

"Lebanon was Child's Play"

"Anything Goes – Except Killing Arafat"

Most West Bank Cities Under Israeli Control

Rajoub's People Surrendered, Handed Over Wanted Individuals

IDF Race Against Time: Four Soldiers Killed

End of the Road for the Man Responsible for Murder of 66 Israelis

IDF in Control of Most of the Jenin Refugee Camp

"People Ran Into the Fire to Pull Out Their Friends"

But *Yediot Ahronot*, in contrast to *Ma'ariv*, does protest against the closure of the battle area to journalists. "Citizens of a democratic country," says the paper in its editorial of April 8, "should not be swallowing information about the heavy fighting fed to them by the army spokesman, and settling for dubious rumors." To compensate for the restrictions, the paper matter-of-factly tries all possible methods. On the one hand, the paper receives reports from correspondent Guy Leshem, who is *on reserve duty* in the territories, a position which totally wipes out any distinction between the subject and the object of reporting (and may be thought of as a preliminary experiment in "embedding"). The paper also negotiates with the army, trying to get correspondents into the area (negotiations that resulted, for example, in the exclusive report from the *muqata'a*). But, on the other hand, *Yediot Ahronot* lets reporter Tsadok Yekhezkeli find ways of his own to get into the war zone, *without* the army's permission – and publishes his reports uncensored. Yekhezkeli, a reporter of the old school, considers the closure mainly as a challenge: he walks along kilometers of bypass roads, dodges IDF checkpoints, and brings in materials of outstanding interest (to which we will return).[4] The commentaries that accompany the reports also tend to moderate the spirit of battle. Here, for instance, is a paragraph from a commentary written by Ronny Shaked, published on page 9 of the March 31 issue, under the headline: "This is Not the Way to Vanquish the Palestinians":

> True, even without the defeat of Ramallah and the siege on Arafat, the Palestinians would have continued their infernal attacks. But yesterday's attack in Tel Aviv, as well as the one in Jerusalem on Friday, are directly connected to Ramallah. They prove that the IDF – with its military superiority, its technology and trained soldiers – can easily move into the cities of the West Bank, but it cannot defeat the Palestinians and it certainly cannot do away with terror.

When Jenin dominates the news, the paper actually offers its readers quite a reasonable coverage of the events. To a large extent, this is the result of Tsadok Yekhezkeli's work. Yekhezkeli entered Jenin without prior clearance from the IDF, via a dirt road used by Palestinians to smuggle food and equipment into the camp. From there he sent in eyewitness reports of the events. An initial report of the events was published on April 14, partly based on Yekhezkeli's materials. The incursion into the refugee camp was mentioned in the front-page headline, under an impressive photograph of the devastation there. Both the headline and the subtitle reflect an Israeli viewpoint, but the tone is neutral and restrained. The headline does not focus on the massacre claim, and the wording acknowledges – if only indirectly – the profound significance of the situation:

Jenin Refugee Camp Concedes Defeat

Following seven days of battle, the last men on the "wanted" list gave themselves up, and the tremendous devastation was revealed. Palestinians: The Israelis conducted a massacre. IDF: They booby-trapped the entire camp. We paid a terrible price too.

The word "too" at the end of the subhead deserves a moment of reflection: without it, the entire sentence would imply a total denial of the Palestinians' claims. *We* have paid a terrible price, therefore *their* claims are unfounded. This is *Ma'ariv*'s strategy, and also the strategy of Israel's official spokesmen. *Yediot Ahronot* presents an "Israeli" perspective which is nevertheless more complex: both sides have paid a terrible price.

On page 4 of the same issue, Yekhezkeli's article appears under the headline "Dozens of Houses Crushed, Hundreds of Homeless Refugees". Two days later, on April 14, a whole double-spread (pages 12 and 13) is dedicated to Yekhezkeli's findings. The headline says: "The Streets are not Strewn with Bodies". The description in the subheadline would be hard to find even in *Ha'aretz*:

> *Yediot Ahronot*'s correspondent managed to enter the refugee camp. An initial visit on the ground revealed a number of facts: The devastation throughout the camp is tremendous, many families are left homeless, without their breadwinner, almost without food; at least thirty bodies are decomposing inside houses, but at this stage there is no evidence of a massacre of civilians.

Two other articles by Yekhezkeli, published on the same pages, add to this grim description. In one of them, residents of the refugee camp are interviewed. The headline reads: "We Will Teach the Children to Hate Jews Even More". The other article is titled: "The Plan that was Stopped: IDF Cooler Vans were Already Stationed on the Camp's Outskirts".

The importance of this article cannot be overestimated, even if only to prove, yet again, that on-the-ground, independent reporting is simply indispensable. The Palestinians saw these vans and claimed that the IDF intended to "clean up" the area and bury the dead before the international press was allowed into the camp. The Israeli establishment immediately denied these claims, and most of the media simply endorsed this statement. (In *Ha'aretz*, as we shall see, reporter Amos Harel wrote about "hints" from IDF sources concerning this delicate issue, but this part of his report was relegated to the end of his article.) Yekhezkeli was there, saw the vans, asked some questions, and dispatched his item, writing "the IDF was concerned that the Palestinians might use the corpses of terrorists who died in the fight in order to argue that the army killed civilians". But he also added that "sources in the IDF said there was no intention of separating civilians from terrorists, it being assumed that the number of civilian corpses would be small". At any rate, it turns out that the Palestinian claim was not so very far from the truth, even if the plan was not actually carried out. The fact that *Yediot Ahronot* published this item, under the above mentioned headline, is significant.

Finally, it was *Yediot Ahronot* that carried the most important story published in the Israeli press about the Jenin events – again by Yekhezkeli. The article, published in the weekend magazine of May 31, told the story of reserve soldier Moshe Nissim, one of the bulldozer operators at the camp. Here is one excerpt from Nissim's account:

> I wanted to wipe out the whole place. I'd sob on the radio, asking the officers to let me wipe them out completely, get it done and get out … For three days I just went on and on, wiping them out. The entire place. I razed every house they shot from. I'd raze a few more to make my way. They were warned by megaphone to get out before I moved in. But I didn't give them a chance. I didn't wait. I didn't hit the house and wait for them to come out. I'd hit the house real hard so that it would go down as fast as possible. I wanted to get it done as quickly as possible, so I could get to other houses, wipe out a lot. Maybe others held back. Or maybe they say they held back. Don't let them fool you. If you were there, if you had seen our soldiers inside the houses, you would understand they were in a death trap. I thought about saving them. I didn't think twice – but I didn't destroy things just for the sake of it. I followed orders in everything. There were many people in the houses we started to tear down. They came out of the houses we entered. I didn't personally see people die under my D-9 [bulldozer], and I didn't see people getting crushed under their houses. But if it had happened, it wouldn't have bothered me at all. I am sure people did die inside these houses, but it was hard to see. There was so much dust, and we often worked in the dark. Every time a house went down I really enjoyed it, because I knew they don't care about dying, they care more about the houses. When you demolish a house you bury 40 or 50 people forever. If I'm upset about anything, it's the fact that we didn't wipe out the whole camp.

The story behind this chilling testimony is just as meaningful as the testimony itself. In the weeks following the Jenin events, the IDF referred the media to a large number of officers and fighters from all types of units, all of whom, as we saw in *Ma'ariv*, made a point of emphasizing their ethical behavior on the ground. At the same time, the IDF systematically prevented exposure of the bulldozer operators. When Yekhezkeli insisted that he wanted to talk to the "D-9ers", as the operators were called (after their bulldozers), he kept hearing the name of one of the operators, whose code name on the radio was *Douby Kourdy* (Kurdish Bear). "I asked to speak to him," says Yekhezkeli, "but they wouldn't let me. They said, 'It's not worth it, let it go.'" Yekhezkeli did not manage to get the man's name, but he did learn that he was a fan of the *Beitar Yerushalayim* soccer team. He asked his sources in Jerusalem to trace the man. Some days later, an acquaintance of his, a taxi driver, called and said he had located the man. Yekhezkeli quickly contacted him and got his testimony. "There was no essential difference between his testimony and the others," Yekhezkeli told me in an interview. "It was only the tone. The things he said were not so different from what others had told me. But *they* were more cautious, more diplomatic. This man did not reflect on the implications of his words, he expressed things in a way that wasn't the standard."

In its April 19 editorial, *Ha'aretz* stated that "in the Israel of 2002, it is hardly possible to cover up atrocities". But the simple truth is that many people in the camp knew about *Douby Kourdy* and what he had done, and would not let Yekhezkeli interview him. They knew very well why. In the Israel of 2002, much like everywhere else, it was quite possible to cover up atrocities. Under such circumstances, the media ought to acknowledge the possibility of such cover-ups, and consider them a professional challenge, regardless of the ideological implications. This was Yekhezkeli's perspective. As far as he was concerned, Nissim was "the most colourful character" on the ground. He simply wanted to meet him and get the interview.

Yediot Ahronot, then, occupies a much more interesting, complex position than *Ma'ariv* during the operation. It strongly criticizes Sharon, and unwaveringly supports the soldiers in the field; it ignores the political opposition almost completely, but offers a rather surprising forum for the extra-parliamentary opposition; it is almost perfectly indifferent to the Palestinian plight throughout the operation, but it does not reject Yekhezkeli's reports from the camp, nor does it relegate them to the back pages. This last distinction, to be sure, is again based on the issue of identity, because *Yediot Ahronot* is not willing to accept such materials from non-Israelis, and it is outraged by very similar accusations against Israel when they come from abroad. In other words, *Yediot Ahronot* shares with *Ma'ariv* the urge to provide Israelis with a defense mechanism against guilt, but it nevertheless distinguishes, at least to some extent, between internal discourse and the discourse of blame coming in from the outside.

HA'ARETZ:
"SHARON GOT INTO OFFICE
THANKS TO ARAFAT'S TERRORISM"

During operation Defensive Shield, *Ha'aretz* can best be described as communicating a sense of *unease*: the paper has a hard time deciding where it wants to position itself with respect to the conflict, and, even more importantly, with respect to the question of guilt. On the one hand, it remains the same newspaper it always was: the style is reserved, the headlines are informative, significant exposure is given to the Palestinian perspective, and the paper generally respects the opposition and offers ample criticism of Sharon's policies. On the other hand, just like the other newspapers, *Ha'aretz* is convinced that Arafat is the single real culprit in this tragic story, and is consequently struggling to reposition itself closer to the *new consensual narrative* of the beginning of the Intifada, the narrative which, more than anything else, asserts that Barak's "generous proposals" at Camp David acquit Israel from any accusation regarding the continuation of the occupation. In a real sense, as I show in *Intifada Hits the Headlines*, *Ha'aretz* is the newspaper which most assiduously followed this narrative at the beginning of the Intifada, and during operation Defensive Shield. It thus fluctuates between its criticism of Sharon and its acceptance of Barak's narrative: if Barak actually proved that there was "no partner on the other side", then, by implication, Sharon is doing the only thing left to do, that is, defend Israel against terror by brute force. The articles dealing with the Palestinian population are thus systematically relegated to the back pages of news section B, which is usually dedicated to *soft* news, and the front pages express cautious support for the military action. The leading front-page commentary on March

31, written by Yoel Marcus, exemplifies this sense of confusion: it starts off with a declaration of support for the operation, then points an accusing finger at Arafat, and ends up with a cautious reminder that Sharon may not be trusted. The occupation is never mentioned. The headline says: "We Know How To Get In":[5]

> The following words may sound trite, but never before have they been as appropriate: no country would tolerate a situation in which its capital, its cities and its towns become the constant target of murderous attacks such as those inflicted on us by the Palestinians ... The suicide attacks, which now involve the Fatah [as well as the other organizations], are perpetrated with the consent, guidance and encouragement of Arafat, who is playing the underdog ... Sharon got into office thanks to Arafat's terrorism and violence. Yet again, as happened throughout his career, he finds himself at a complicated junction, with military actions evolving in ways which do not always lead to a happy end ... In Sharon's case, the problem with an unfolding operation is that there is no way of knowing where it will lead ... You cannot expect much of a war, unless you can present a political alternative.

In line with this perspective, *Ha'aretz* explicitly questions the operation's goals, and touches on the sensitive issue of the decision-making process in the government – but makes a point of doing all this in the inner pages, never on the front page. Here are some of the headlines which, in different circumstances, could have made it to the front page of the paper:

The Goals of the Military Action Remain Unclear

Sharon Surprised by Resistance Against Expulsion of Arafat

Sharon Tries to Gain Time Before International Intervention

The paper's policy with respect to the opposition is similar. Headlines which reflect oppositionary views appear quite frequently in the inner pages, but do not make it to the front page. Note that as opposed to the two other papers, these headlines do not mock the opposition, but give it a respectable platform:

Conscientious Objector: I Am Willing to
Serve in Any Defensive War

Meretz: IDF's Extensive Activity in the Territories
Will Only Encourage Terrorism

Dozens of Demonstrators Support Palestinians in Arab Towns

"Peace Coalition" Promises a Flurry of Demonstrations

"We Must Prevent Further Losses", Say Widows

Unlike *Yediot Ahronot*, *Ha'aretz*'s editorials do not mention the ban on journalists during the entire operation. But on April 5, a front-page headline announces: "IDF Considers Letting Israeli Press Into Territories". Like his colleague from *Ma'ariv*, the paper's military correspondent, Amos Harel, wavers between his concern for the freedom of the press and his wish to help the IDF forces in the field defend themselves against accusations coming in from the outside. This, for example, is what he writes on April 9:

A quick visit to the Kasbah [in Nablus] yesterday, during the last hours of fighting there, showed the IDF in a very different light than the way it has been recently portrayed: a professional, efficient army taking on an extremely complex mission, and investing a lot of thought and caution. From this perspective, Israel's information campaign seems more misguided than ever ... Even yesterday, the few journalists who did get in reached the site by means of their own. And even then, they were allowed to join the forces only if they took no pictures. They were further instructed that all interviews would be strictly off the record. This smokescreen policy has created the feeling that the IDF has something to hide. But the paratroopers in Nablus do not feel they need to be ashamed. They are actually proud.

Significantly, the paper does not complain about the foreign press coverage of the events, and it occasionally publishes reports about foreign correspondents' complaints about IDF restrictions. In this sense, the paper does not project the sense of hostility towards the foreign press which, in the other newspapers, accompanies the attempt to suppress guilt. Moreover, and this is crucial, the paper takes no part in the effort to construct a sense of support for the soldiers and the reservists. On April 2, the paper's front page carries a photograph of a reserve soldier taking leave of his girlfriend, and only a single article dealing with the reserve units' mobilization appears on April 10, under the headline "More

People Than Required Turned Up For Reserve Service, But No One Agreed to Leave". In fact, the paper's lack of interest in the reserve units is almost puzzling. *Ha'aretz* does not deal with their economic hardship, with the long-term separation from their families, the fears of their children, or the hardships of keeping their civilian lives in some kind of shape. More than anything else, this should be understood as a fact about identity: *Ha'aretz* positions itself as the newspaper of the elite, and the type of social identity that it projects is that of well-to-do, upper middle-class, well-educated, Western-oriented Jewish Israelis. *Ha'aretz* seems to assume, then, that not too many members of this class were recruited as reservists at the beginning of the operation.

How does *Ha'aretz* cover the ongoing operation on the ground? The paper uses every editorial means at its disposal to make it clear that it covers the events from an *Israeli* perspective. There is absolutely no resemblance between the paper's framing of the events and that of the foreign media: *Ha'aretz* does not report an Israeli "incursion" into the Palestinian Authority's territory – it reports a war conducted by the IDF against the roots of terror in the territories. Most of the large, front-page headlines tell the story from the IDF's viewpoint:

Arafat's Office Under Siege; Seven Israelis Killed During the Weekend

IDF Will Have to Move Quickly

IDF Enters Nablus; Surrounds Armed Palestinians in Bethlehem's Church of Nativity

Suspected Robbers and Murderers Caught During West Bank Action

The Shubaki Document: Fatah Members Demanded Authority's Funding for Suicide Attacks

Wanted Men Under Siege at Rajoub Headquarters; IDF Enters Bethlehem and Tulkarem

The Battle in Jenin Refugee Camp – Toughest Confrontation Since the Start of Defensive Shield

IDF: Adwan Was Responsible for the Deaths of At Least 74 Israelis

15 Soldiers Killed in Jenin and Nablus;
IDF Prepares to Stop West Bank Action

Operation Officers Watched the Battle Helplessly:
"Whoever Raised his Head was Shot"

At the same time, *Ha'aretz* consistently supplies its readership
with significant information about the state of affairs on the
Palestinian side, along with a reasonable presentation of the
Palestinian perspective on the events. From time to time, the
paper actually publishes an item of the type the IDF would not
like to see in print. In this sense, *Ha'aretz* is still in a league of
its own, by far the most substantial source in Hebrew for news
about the other side. This is most clearly signified by Amira Hass's
daily reports and Gideon Levy's weekly column. But this, as I
have already indicated, is only one part of the story. The other
side is that very little critical coverage finds its way to the front
pages. Levi's column is published in the weekly magazine, and
Hass's reports all too often appear in section B of the paper, or
in the inner news pages – never on the front page – with small
headlines:

Ramallah Residents Stocked up on Pitta Bread and Canned Food

Eyewitnesses: IDF Delayed Transport of the Injured in Ramallah

IDF Soldiers Broadcast Pornographic Films on Local TV Stations,
by Mistake

Only Children Dare Go Out and Play on the Desolate Streets
of the Refugee Camp

Due to Ramallah Action: Thousands Disconnected from Water
and electricity

Ramallah Residents Forced to Collect Water from Gutters

Jenin Residents: IDF Pulled Down Houses With People
Still Inside Them

Further Evidence: IDF Uses Palestinians to Search Suspect Houses

In all this, *Ha'aretz* sends its readers a complex message: on
the one hand, the paper accentuates its own commitment to

democratic values; on the other hand, it also indicates quite strongly that with respect to the factual bottom line – *who did what to whom, when and why* – it prefers to go along with the perspective of the Israeli establishment. This is the perspective which consistently makes the front page. *Ha'aretz* is making a statement about itself – it is a liberal, democratic and progressive newspaper – but it is also making a statement about reality. Palestinian claims, generally, do not quite count as serious news. Moreover, and no less importantly, *Ha'aretz* is aware of the fact that many Israelis think of the newspaper as another participant in the discourse of blame against Israel (an attitude expressed, as we saw, by *Ma'ariv*), and is thus trying to minimize the damage. It publishes the reports, but makes sure to annnounce that they only represent a perspective, a viewpoint, which the paper itself does not necessarily adopt.

This complex attitude is dramatically revealed in the paper's coverage of the events in Jenin. *Ha'aretz* publishes quite a few critical reports from the refugee camp, and their distribution in the paper is fascinating. Reports originating from within the IDF, or reflecting the Israeli perspective, appear on the front page, or the main news pages. Thus, for example, the first report about Jenin by military correspondent Amos Harel appears on the front page, under the headline: "Two Soldiers Killed in Jenin Fighting; Criticism Within the IDF: 'We've Sewn Appalling Devastation'". In the text itself, Harel writes:

> IDF officers were shocked with the way the action in Jenin was conducted. "Because of the risks involved, the soldiers hardly make any progress on foot," they said. "The bulldozers simply 'raze' the houses, causing frightful devastation. When the world gets to see what we have been doing there, it will be tremendously damaging to us. The Palestinians in the camp are conducting their own 'Massada' struggle. This is our fault, in part. If we had prepared properly, the situation would be different."

In another article, printed on April 4, and headed "Only Those Who Play by IDF Rules Get Into the Area", Harel writes: "Until yesterday, even though the fighting in the camp was already subsiding, the army would not let the Israeli press in. IDF sources even suggested that the army intends to 'clean up' the site before it pulls out." And so we find the arguments concerning the attempt to "clean up" the site popping up not only in the Palestinian propaganda, but in allegations made by sources inside the IDF.

Harel visited the camp after it was opened to the press, and his report appears on the front page of the April 15 issue, under the headline: "No Evidence of Massacre in the Alleys; The Ruins Have not Yet Been Scanned". The headline does not reflect Harel's harrowing description in the article itself:

> The one incontrovertible fact is the enormous devastation caused by the action in Jenin. A rectangular area in the north-eastern section of the camp, about 100 meters long, and almost as wide, reminded me more than anything else of pictures of the terrible earthquakes in Turkey in recent years. This is where the armed Palestinians put up their main resistance. Until Tuesday morning, when 13 reservists died in a skirmish in a nearby alley, the IDF was advancing carefully. But from that moment, the gloves were off. One house, from which shots were fired, was simply swept aside by the bulldozers. By the end of the action, dozens of houses in this rectangle were likewise erased.

But when Amira Hass sends *her* first report from the camp, it is published on April 19 in section B of the paper, far from the news pages. The report is an extremely harsh account of the IDF's action in the camp. Hass tells the story of a 51-year-old Palestinian man, Abu-Ra'eed, who for five days was forced to open the doors to houses, while IDF soldiers hid behind his back. At night, she adds, he was handcuffed and guarded by two IDF soldiers. She also tells the story of a Palestinian woman, Um-Yasser, who saved a year-old baby from her neighbors' shelled house, and of houses which were destroyed without their residents being warned. None of this finds its way into the news pages.

This, however, is not the end of the story. Much more significant is the way the paper itself, *in its editorial*, refers to Hass's report. Under the headline "There was No Massacre in Jenin", the paper makes the following statement:

In the past few days, journalists – including *Ha'aretz* correspondents – have entered the Jenin refugee camp. They have seen the situation for themselves, and have talked to eyewitnesses about the IDF's activities. Correspondent Amira Hass spent a few days in the camp, and brought in an extensive article, published in this issue. The accounts about the battles in the camp are gruelling, but at this early stage, we should cautiously emphasize what did *not* happen in Jenin: there was no massacre. No order to that effect was given or executed, nor was there any local initiative for the intentional, systematic killing of non-combatants.

In the Israel of 2002, it is hardly possible to cover up atrocities. The accounts of fighters and the officers who fought in Jenin – many of whom are citizens called in for reserve duty for this action – as well as those who observed the events by a variety of means, contradict the accusations about a massacre. The fighting in Jenin was heavy ... and under these circumstances citizens, too, were injured. This is a terrible and sad fact, which results from the nature of war, and in certain specific cases it will be necessary to investigate whether everything possible was done in order to avoid accidental injury to civilians. But labeling the Jenin battle as a "massacre" is erroneous when done by naive people, and misleading when done by others.

The Palestinian propaganda has made despicable use of unfounded tales, some of which were invented outside Jenin. This propaganda was generated by members of the Palestinian Authority who raised false accusations about "executions", in order to fuel hatred against Israel.

This paper's editors, then, use Hass's "extensive article" – which they themselves relegated to the back pages – as part of an argument which starts by determining that there was no massacre, goes on with the notion of "accidental injuries" caused by the "heavy fighting", and ends up with the Palestinians "fuel[ing] hatred against Israel". The highlighting of Amira Hass's article in the editorial is thus eventually used as part of a rhetorical move which ends up with nothing but the suppression of guilt.

This is extremely important, because *Ha'aretz* plays a unique role in Israeli society. It serves as the self-appointed mark of a liberal, democratic, left-oriented stance. It promises to provide its readership with "progressive", "serious", "deep" coverage. The fact that the newspaper conveys a sense of confusion which centers exactly around the issue of guilt, is by far the best illustration of the dramatic shift of consciousness experienced at the beginning of the Intifada by what came to be known as the "confused Left" – the majority of traditional voters of the Labor Party who found themselves convinced by Barak's propagandist claims. Barak's own rhetoric, during his short period in power and afterwards, was explicitly, and many times embarrassingly, obsessed with the notion of guilt. He kept explaining, time after time, that his "experiment" – the "generous proposal" – was designed to bring about one of the two goals: either achieve the "end of the conflict", or, alternatively, release Israel, once and for all, from the burden of guilt. *Ha'aretz*, even more than the other newspapers, accepted this conceptual frame, an acceptance which translated into a clear change in editorial policy. The new policy combined a critical stand towards Sharon with an "understanding", so to speak, that Sharon must function in a world in which it is already clear that the Palestinians are "not ready for peace". *Ha'aretz*'s editors occasionally rationalized this change of policy by pointing to economic factors: many readers, they argued, were cancelling their subscriptions because the paper was projecting a leftist perspective. Such considerations may have indeed played a certain role (we saw how *Ma'ariv* helped create such an impression), but as it turned out, the paper's *publisher*, Amos Schocken, had actually been trying to push for a more critical attitude, while the senior editors were intent on providing their readers with an "updated" perspective. It is difficult to find another case in the history of the modern press where editors push for a more consensual, less critical policy – *against* the publisher's position. This strongly suggests that financial issues are not necessarily at the root of the matter.

Interestingly, in the course of the last three years, *Ha'aretz* has gone through a dramatic upheaval. At first, after operation Defensive Shield, the paper continued to develop its new policy. Amira Hass's news reports were gradually, and after a while almost entirely, removed from the front news pages. Instead, the paper published reports by correspondent Arnon Regular, who focused on the Palestinian Authority. Then, Aviv Lavi's regular column, "I saw, I heard", which systematically and critically investigated the ideological outlines of the Israeli media throughout the Intifada, was cancelled. Instead, the paper published a weekly double-spread which was dedicated, each week, to a different Israeli *family*. This move from critical reporting to consensual identity-politics reflected the new policy in no uncertain terms. In February 2004, however, publisher Schoken dramatically announced that he decided to replace the paper's chief editor, Hanoch Marmari, with the editor of the English-language edition, David Landau – a clear indication that Schoken wanted to see the paper resuming a more critical role. Since April 2004, this indeed seems to be happening.

4
"Live from the Jenin Area": The Television News Broadcasts

On March 29 2002, the first day of operation Defensive Shield, the news broadcasts on Channel 1 and Channel 2 make it clear that these are indeed special days – that now is the time to put aside the regular political debates, and concentrate on the task ahead, the task of "defending our very homes". They convey an almost festive sense of authority, express contained fury about the Netanya terror attack, and do their best to create a sense of unity and wide popular support for the soldiers in the field, and those who are being called for reserve duty.

There is, however, a significant difference in *style* between the two channels, a difference in tone of voice, in the body language of the anchors in the studio, in the language of the commentators – a difference which eventually says something of importance about identity. On Channel 2, the commercial channel, anchor Miki Haimovitch opens the broadcast with the following words:

> Good evening to you all. We had wished you a happy and quiet Passover, but this year's Passover has not been quiet, and it definitely has not been happy. Twenty people were murdered in a suicide attack in Netanya, yesterday. It seems that the sentence in our Hagada – "in every generation they have risen against us to annihilate us" – has not rung so true for many years.

The resemblance to *Ma'ariv*'s headline of the following morning is unmistakable. Haimovitch intimately connects the people at the studio with the audience at home ("*We* have wished *you* a happy and quiet Passover"), and ceremoniously declares that in this generation, too, "*they* have risen against *us* to annihilate us". She returns to the Hagada in the second part of the broadcast, this time in a grim conversation with Israel's Chief Rabbi, Rabbi Israel Lau:

Haimovitch: A massacre of Jews on Passover eve ... Tonight, the sentence "he brought us forth from bondage to freedom" obviously raises a few thoughts ...
Rabbi Lau: Even before this Seder in Netanya, the Hagada had been drenched in tears. Yesterday it was also drenched with bloodstains.

This, to be sure, is hardly an atmosphere conducive to inquiry about the objectives of the military operation just embarked on by the IDF. When Haimovitch asks military correspondent Ronny Daniel how the IDF plans to react, Daniel presents her, and the audience, with an almost euphoric description:

There will be an IDF action. The guiding principle will be: whatever the Palestinians won't do – that is, won't prevent – will have to be prevented by the IDF. The directives are: there is no intention to harm Arafat, no intention to topple the Palestinian Authority – but other than these two negatives, almost anything will be allowed in order to stop this wave of terror.

The parallel edition on Channel 1, the state-owned channel, projects a very different atmosphere. It is much less emotional, and expresses a noticeable strain of doubt. Unlike Haimovitch, anchor Gilad Adin overcomes the temptation to elucidate the significance of the Netanya attack by a reference to the Hagada. Instead, he opens the newscast, in a matter-of-fact tone, with the following news summary:

Following the murderous terror attack in Netanya, the IDF is moving large numbers of troops in Judea and Samaria. The government will convene for a special deliberation about the response to this attack, and the security services are preparing a wide-ranging action in the Palestinian Authority's areas of jurisdiction. The Palestinians are on alert.

Military correspondent Amir Bar Shalom then presents his report, which he ends up, in direct opposition to Daniel, with a *question*:

In the discussions held at the Ministry of Defense in the last 24 hours, the IDF proposed a number of courses of action, all of which essentially involve re-entering the territories currently under Palestinian rule. The question now is, how forceful Israel's reaction will be, and whether it will be effective this time.

The difference between the two openings of these broadcasts does not spell a radical difference in perspective with respect to the *news*. As we shall see, both channels have much in common in terms of their analysis of reality. The difference between the openings is at another level, that of the relationship between the news, the people at the studio, and the people at home. On Channel 1, Adin and Bar Shalom maintain a certain distance between themselves and the object of the coverage, and between themselves and their audience. They project a certain formality: Adin is there to summarize the news, and Bar Shalom is there to present his reports. On Channel 2, this collapses into an emotional, excited discourse of identity. Haimovitch is there to represent the people at home, to give them a voice, to reflect, to acknowledge, what *they* feel, while Daniel is there to send them an encouraging message: almost everything that can be done will be done to stop this wave of terror.

This is how most of Channel 2's broadcasts look during operation Defensive Shield. The news reports are framed as a means to communicate identity, self-image, collective emotions. As we shall see, when the anchors approach their reporters with questions, they always start with an expression such as "The people at home must be asking themselves ...". Most of the commentary on the broadcasts, especially by the commentator for Arab Affairs, Ehud Ya'ari, projects a contemptuous, hostile position towards the Palestinian Authority, especially towards Arafat, and complete denial of any claims coming in from the other side. The channel does broadcast short reports from the territories, but they are systematically relegated to the second half of the edition, usually after the commercial break. This simple editorial practice sends a clear message to the audience: not unlike *Ha'aretz*, the channel acknowledges the other side's right to represent itself, but it also declares that it refuses to take what the Palestinians say into account in the framing of the news.

The news reports on Channel 1 are much less consistent. On some evenings, when the question of guilt hovers heavily over the events on the ground, the news looks and sounds exactly as it does on Channel 2. On other evenings, Channel 1 manages to keep a distance from the objects of coverage and from the audience. On these evenings, it quotes more Palestinian sources, broadcasts more troubling visuals from the field, and maintains a significantly critical stand – both with respect to the military operation and with respect to the government's policy.

As we have already pointed out, the overall perspectives projected by the two channels have a lot in common. Both spend a lot of time expressing undivided support for the soldiers in the field, and neither provides the political opposition with a suitable platform.[1] Even more importantly, both channels make an effort to conceal the fact that the IDF closed the territories to journalists during the first phase of the operation. The anchors never inform their viewers that what they are watching is second-hand material provided by the IDF, and they sometimes present these materials as if they are broadcast live "from the ground". Channel 1 correspondents often appear on screen, live, standing near the IDF's vehicles parked outside the prohibited area. They often wear bulletproof vests. The anchors' presentation follows a formula which became routine during the operation's first days: "Our correspondent has spent the day in the Bethlehem – or Qalqilya, or Jenin – *area*." Strictly speaking, of course, this is not a lie, but it is highly misleading, and when this formulation joins the live broadcast, the bulletproof vest, and the reporter's tone, it creates the impression that the reporter is truly where the action is taking place. This occurs much less frequently on Channel 2, where Ronny Daniel usually broadcasts from the studio. But his reports are misleading in a different way: sitting in the studio, he describes events occurring deep inside the territories – descriptions which are, of course, entirely based on military sources. However, his words are accompanied by visual material that could be obtained without getting into the closed area: army convoys within Israel, panoramic long-distance shots of Palestinian towns, helicopters circling in the air, and video materials shot and edited by the IDF's spokesman. This combination creates an impression of authenticity, and because the media exclusion is never explicitly mentioned, it is difficult, almost impossible, for viewers to figure out that this is not really a report from the field.

Interestingly, however, Channel 1's reporters do mention the media exclusion more than once – not as the topic of the report, but still, in a tone that is not uncritical. On Channel 2, no such comments are heard. Here, for instance, is Channel 1's correspondent Gur Tsalal-Yachin, in two different reports, on April 1 and April 7:

> The IDF is not only fighting the Palestinians – it is clashing with the media too. It turns out, that the soldiers' guidelines are not clear. More than once soldiers tried to prevent our work even when there was no real limitation.

> The IDF will not let us enter Jenin, and so it is hard to know what is really happening in the refugee camp.

This difference between the two channels becomes much more pronounced when it touches on the IDF's campaign against the foreign and Palestinian media. On April 12, for example, Channel 1 broadcasts a very reasonable story about the difficulties encountered by foreign correspondents, and in the course of the month its reporters bring in several accounts by foreign colleagues, who managed to get to places where the Israeli correspondents themselves could not enter. Channel 2, on the other hand, explicitly complains about the foreign media, and expresses some satisfaction when their movements are impeded. Here, for instance, is commentator Ehud Ya'ari, talking with anchor Miki Haimovitch, on April 10:

> *Ya'ari*: As far as the Jenin refugee camp is concerned, Israel is facing a public relations challenge of the first order ... The other side is talking about the destruction of 30 per cent of the houses in the camp ... They are talking about a total number of 500 dead in Nablus and Jenin ... and supposed executions of people who had surrendered. This creates a situation which Israel must respond to immediately – not tomorrow morning or towards the end of the week, but right now, because this sort of thing snowballs.
> *Haimovich*: And to this we must add the images they plan to show the world once we get out of there, of dozens and hundreds of bodies, and the destroyed houses and everything ...
> *Ya'ari*: As of now, the IDF has managed to put a complete halt on the work of Palestinian photographers in the territories. This is the case now, and for the past few days, and it wasn't simple to do.

And, on April 18, Ronny Daniel brings in some comments from an IDF briefing for foreign correspondents, then zooms in on a CNN correspondent and adds "The foreign media has heard [the Israeli position] with considerable suspicion ... Here is CNN's correspondent, who is quick to state the facts even before IDF officers have finished their presentation."

This wide gap between the two channels' perspectives on the foreign media lies at the heart of the matter: Channel 2 consistently projects a hostile, defensive attitude towards those who are most readily associated with the discourse of blame against Israel. As commentator Ya'ari puts it, the issue is "a public affairs challenge of the first order". Channel 1, at least to some extent, detaches itself from the discourse of blame: it identifies itself as a media organization, puts a certain distance between itself and the government establishment, and criticizes the IDF for interfering with the foreign correspondents' work.

This type of critical stand manifests itself in other domains as well. Thus, for example, Channel 1's senior commentators Oded Granot and Amnon Abramovitch consistently express their doubts regarding Sharon's future plans. On March 29, for example, they concentrate on what they call the question of "future vision": does Sharon have a clear vision of a political program for the moment after the end of the military action? Granot wonders whether declaring Arafat an enemy actually prevents any future return to the diplomatic process. And towards the end of the broadcast, Abramovitch sums up the situation as follows: "When you embark on an operation like this, you also need a future vision. I don't know what's going on in the Prime Minister's head, as far as this is concerned. I really want to believe that he knows."

On the March 28 broadcast, Channel 1's military analyst, Ron Ben-Yishay, has the following to say about the goals of the operation:

> In the IDF, there are also people who say: either we go for the real thing, that is, a temporary occupation of the territories in order to uproot terrorism and arrest wanted individuals ... or we go for targeted actions based on intelligence information ... Major action which will once again send wanted individuals to look for shelter in places the IDF cannot reach, is the sort

of thing that will only increase the Palestinians' motivation for terror.

This, to be sure, is not radical criticism. Originating from within the army, it deals with the operational *method* to be used by the IDF. The fact of the matter, however, is that even this type of criticism cannot be found on Channel 2. In the following conversation, for example, from the March 29 broadcast, Channel 2 anchors Gady Sukenik and Miki Haimovitch make a rare attempt to ask reporter Ronny Daniel a relatively critical question about the IDF's mode of operation (note how Sukenik presents his question on behalf of the *people*, and how both Sukenik and Daniel use the lice metaphor to refer to Palestinian terrorists):

> *Daniel*: Capturing a city in the current configuration is not what it used to be in the past ... The job is based on intelligence, targeting people, places, arms stacks, anybody who's involved in terrorism – they are trying to get all of these out of Ramallah with a very, very fine comb ...
>
> *Sukenik*: But Ronny, excuse me, the question is – and many people must be asking themselves – didn't we do the same not so long ago? We moved out and returned, so what's the difference? We're combing through the same hair, again and again – actually, what's the difference?
>
> *Daniel*: It's not the same, Gady, this time the incursion looks different, it's meant to be different. Last time we entered Ramallah, the plan was to get a message through. Now there are no more messages – now it's action, and with its scope and depth – again, no total success is promised – it can definitely decrease (with time, not immediately, judging by the number of alerts more terror attacks are quite possible tomorrow and the day after), but with time it is quite clearly possible that actions of this type will decrease the level of terror, and that, after all, is the point.
>
> *Haimovitch*: Did they take into account that this long stay may cause Israeli casualties, the type of bog we were caught up in Lebanon?
>
> *Daniel*: I don't think that using this image of the Lebanese bog is quite appropriate at present. Definitely, this has been taken into account, Miki ... but there's no other option, apparently.[2]

BROADCASTING INNOCENCE: TWO CHANNELS, ONE VOICE

The news on Channel 1, as I have already indicated, does not always maintain its critical edge. On April 9, for example, it does not. This is no coincidence. On that day, 13 IDF soldiers were killed in Jenin. From the Israeli point of view, it was the worst day of the operation. Like Channel 2, Channel 1 generates an almost totally co-opted broadcast. Both channels allow only a brief, marginal glimpse of the Palestinian side, and both concentrate on a single message, a message which is, explicitly and directly, about guilt: the 13 soldiers were killed *because* they made a special effort to avoid harming Palestinian civilians at the camp, and their deaths are thus proof of the IDF's high moral standards.

The Channel 2 news broadcast opens with a long, dramatic report by Ronny Daniel, including lengthy excerpts from a briefing with Major General Yitzhak Eytan, Head of Central Command, and visual materials provided by the army's spokesman. Daniel then goes on to describe the events as they unfold in real time – from the point of view of the soldiers in the field. He himself is located "in the Jenin *area*":

> All the signs show that fighting continues over there, all with the purpose of getting to the very last corner, the last people – according to evaluations there are now about 100 armed people, from Islamic Jihad and Hamas, who are still barricaded, and willing – as they loudly announce – to kill themselves while attacking soldiers ... The fighting goes on, and I believe the end is still far away.

Commentator Ehud Ya'ari then appears on the screen, and presents what, from his point of view, counts as the Palestinian perspective on "this tough day of fighting": "Beyond the obvious – that they will turn Jenin into a myth, a story of heroism, about the birth of the new Palestinian fighter – these things could be anticipated; beyond this, I would say that the main point is this: Arafat keeps raising the stakes."

At this stage, anchor Miki Haimovitch introduces the topic of the day. "Fighting in populated areas," she says, "of the type that took place today in Jenin, is considered particularly complex. Soldiers have to fight against fighters who are hiding inside homes, while trying to avoid injuries to civilians ... Here is Moshe Nussbaum's report." Nussbaum, in regular times the correspondent on police affairs, shows footage of IDF soldiers using megaphones to call on the Palestinians to surrender "in order to ensure their safety". The IDF, says Nussbaum, was interested in "avoiding real fighting", but "the fighting was eventually imposed on the troops". Nussbaum spends some time explaining the operational complexities of fighting in populated areas, and then goes on to make the point of the report:

> To all these problems, we must add the moral difficulty experienced by the soldiers in almost all the towns and villages they have entered: the fact that the terrorists have positioned themselves inside homes and have surrounded themselves with innocent civilians.

An expert witness is then summoned to the studio, to comment on this "moral difficulty". The witness is no other than Ehud Yatom, the former Head of Operations at the *Shin-Bet* (Secret Service). In 1984, in what came to be known as the "Bus No. 300 Affair", Yatom executed two Palestinian terrorists who kidnapped a bus on its way from Tel Aviv to Ashkelon. The terrorists were captured, handcuffed, interrogated, and then killed on the spot. Almost twenty years later, Yatom says: "Our ethics are irreproachable. If we had used helicopters and air force, I think we would have spared ourselves – I wouldn't say all, but a great part of – the casualties."

Major General Eytan, in another excerpt from his briefing, then repeats the very same message: "The entire area is mingled with a passive, civilian population – women, children, old people, women [*sic*]. And action from the air would have taken a very high toll in terms of people who do not participate in the fighting." This is immediately repeated, yet again, by reporter Ronny Daniel: "There were helicopters on the scene as well, but, we repeat, since there are still civilians in some of the houses – and it is not clear in which – this is what gets in the way of using artillery, or planes, for example, and not just helicopters."

The wordings, of course, are significant. Major General Eytan describes the area as "mingled with" civilians; according to Nussbaum, "the terrorists surrounded themselves with innocent citizens"; Daniel adds that "in some of the houses, and it is not clear in which", civilians are still present. Language is harnessed here to obfuscate the basic fact that these civilians simply *live* in the refugee camp, that it is their home, and it is this home of theirs which has been forcefully invaded by the IDF – for reasons which may or may not be considered justified.

Then, towards the end of this part of the edition, two very short reports are broadcast from the Palestinian town of Tulkarem, by reporters Yoram Binur and Erez Rotem. They, too, focus mainly on the IDF's perspective, but they also indicate that the Palestinians have a slightly different view of things. Binur says:

> We can now see the heavy price the Palestinians have had to pay ... The destruction here is hard to watch, almost all the buildings were damaged. Water, electricity and telephone infrastructures are out of service, and the Palestinian first-aid services are almost non-functional.

Rotem reports that "the Palestinians claim the soldiers also caused severe damage to homes", and immediately switches to one of the soldiers, who says "No, it is not true, we cleaned up their houses afterwards, with bleach, and all kinds of stuff ... We gave them provisions, gave them provisions we got for ourselves." All this, to be sure, does very little in terms of the overall framing of the news.

Turning our attention to the parallel broadcast on Channel 1, we start at around mid-program, when anchor Haim Yavin asks reporter Keren Neubach how Israel is preparing to cope with Palestinian accusations about a massacre in Jenin. "Well", says Neubach:

> [Foreign Minister] Peres says the Palestinians will try to say – they will try to say there was a massacre in Jenin. We, Israel, will have to explain that what happened there was not a massacre, but simply very tough combat against people who are all armed, most of them potential suicide bombers, and the sad evidence for this is the large number of Israeli casualties.

This, to be sure, is a reasonable presentation of Peres' words, but the significant point is that almost everything in the broadcast, before and after Neubach's comment, is dedicated to this very attempt "to explain" – *to explain away the sense of guilt*.

The broadcast begins with correspondent Gur Tsalal-Yachin reporting "from the ground", somewhere near Jenin, and moves on directly to Major General Eytan's briefing. "Action from the air," says the general, "would have taken a very high toll on people who are not involved in the fighting, so the solution of using air force and heavy shelling is impossible in this type of fighting." Correspondent Amir Bar Shalom then repeats the very same words: "The option of a massive attack from the air was discarded because of the concern about civilian casualties", a comment which is immediately followed by another excerpt from General Eytan: "Unfortunately, these terrorists don't show any concern for their own civilian population, and they use them as a living shield in order to fight us." A little later, anchor Yavin asks commentator Ron Ben-Yishay about the heavy casualties in Jenin, and Ben-Yishay, visibly moved, replies as follows:

> What causes the really heavy losses is the fact that IDF soldiers cannot use the air force or bulldozers, for fear of hurting the innocent civilian population. That's the basic, fundamental reason for the IDF's losses in the camp – not just in this camp, but elsewhere too. Because I have seen how the Russians did it in Grozny: they simply razed a town of 40,000 people. The IDF doesn't do this, and so it takes losses.

Is the message clear? Not yet, apparently. In the second part of the edition, a lengthy interview is aired with Major Ilan, an infantry officer who was injured in the action and hospitalized in Haifa. Most of the interview focuses on the very same issue. This is what Major Ilan has to say:

> We didn't start fighting yesterday. From the moment we left Lebanon, a year and a half ago, our orders were to get ready. My first training was in combat in populated areas, full of civilians, with terrorists inside. When we enter these places, we know how to separate the civilians, put them in a safe place, on the side, and then we go on fighting. It makes things difficult, but we cope with it. Unlike the terrorists we face, of course, who are using the civilian population and sometimes even get help from them, whether it is to find hiding places or to shoot from houses with people inside them. What you have there are not normal fighters, at least not the kind of fighters I know. There are individuals there who often act like people about to commit

suicide … maybe they're even on drugs … not in a reasonable and normal way.

And as on Channel 2, this sequence is interrupted only once, when correspondent Moshe Cohen reports from two West Bank towns:

> The centre of Nablus today looks like a city after an earthquake. The damage is severe. Torn-up roads, shattered windows, bullet-scarred buildings. Tanks are moving through the streets of the town, which is under curfew … These images, shot yesterday, were broadcast worldwide today: the evacuation of the dead and injured from the combat zone in the *kasbah*. The Palestinians estimate that they have lost over forty people in the fighting here, but these numbers are not final. Today, the images of devastation are coming in from the center of the Qalqilya as well. Citizens are returning to routine life, following the IDF's withdrawal from the town. Many people are rushing to the stores to buy food.

On April 9, then, both editions are nearly identical – and for the most part dedicated to the argument that leads from the death of the soldiers to the moral innocence of the IDF. This, however, is not always the case.

BETWEEN IDENTITY AND INVESTIGATION:
TWO CHANNELS, TWO VOICES

The news broadcasts on April 12, a day in which a major suicide bombing took place near the Machane-Yehuda market in Jerusalem, provide a good example of the significant difference between both channels. Channel 1, which does not even attempt to provide a critical perspective on a day in which the major topic is one of guilt, produces a very different type of coverage on a day in which the issue of guilt does not arise, a day in which a suicide bombing simply and clearly situates Israelis on the side of the victims.

On Channel 2, the news begins, as usual, with short and definitive proclamations of the "broadcast's headlines", by Ronny Daniel, Ehud Ya'ari and political correspondent Udi Segal:

Ronny Daniel: The IDF will continue its operation in the territories, they do not feel any pressure. I think that the Americans, too, have settled for the Prime Minister's very loose definition, which says "we will be done as soon as possible." At this point the action is entering the more effective stages ... people are being captured and interrogated, intelligence is being gathered, the action against the infrastructure of terror continues, and this will go on; there is no sense of American pressure, certainly not in any aggressive way. And one more thing, which already has to do with the day after: this operation creates a totally new state of affairs. The IDF did indeed go into the territories in order to enter a town, shake things up, get a hold on terror there – but it seems to me that the new reality on the ground, now that the Palestinian Authority has ceased to exist as an entity for all practical purposes, is that the IDF will stay in these territories, in one way or another, at least to some extent. Even when it will pull out of the towns, it will not actually move out of there. And the situation on the ground is, let us put it this way, a kind of redistribution of the area, with the IDF everywhere.

Ehud Ya'ari: The Palestinians, Arafat, are telling the Americans: If you think you will pressure us into surrendering and accepting conditions for a ceasefire, you are wasting your time. The same message is also conveyed by the fact that Fatah has shown no hesitation whatsoever in claiming responsibility for today's attack.

Udi Segal: Sharon's offer to [Secretary of State] Powell this morning is: "Gaza first". The Palestinian security forces' attitude will be tested here. Take Gaza, we didn't go in, we didn't touch it. They have security forces there, the Palestinian Authority wasn't crushed there – fine, if Arafat really is serious about his intentions, let this be the test case. Defense Minister Ben Eliezer is telling Powell: Don't believe Arafat when he tells you he cannot do anything. After this operation, the *Tanzim* [the PLO combat units] is the strongest force on the ground.

There is nothing here which even tries to go beyond the uncritical representation of the government's official position. As far as Ronny Daniel is concerned, the fact that "the Palestinian Authority has ceased to exist as an entity for all practical purposes" is *not* a result of the Israeli action, and it definitely has nothing to do with the *goals* of the entire operation. The IDF entered the territory in order to "get a hold on terror there", and then "a new reality" emerged "on the ground", which seems to require the IDF's continued presence there, "in one way or another, at least to some extent". Ya'ari's perspective regarding the Palestinian side amounts to the notion that they, the Palestinians, simply continue sending violent messages to the Americans, and suicide bombers to Jerusalem. Udi Segal, for his part, invests the claims made by Sharon and Ben Eliezer – which, by the way, flatly contradict Ronny Daniel's observations – with factual status: Arafat can do everything, and his willingness to stop the violence is going to be tested yet again. A few other short items are then aired, followed by a special report from Ramallah, by correspondent Itay Engel. In the past, Engel has actually brought in a series of rather daring, critical reports from the territories. The last of these reports, broadcast a few weeks before the operation, included a few negative comments from soldiers, which infuriated Defense Minister Ben Eliezer, and, according to some sources, directly influenced his decision to close the area to journalists at the beginning of the operation. Now, Engel goes back to the battleground, joins an IDF force in action in Ramallah, and presents a report which is nothing but a long argument for the moral responsibility of the IDF and its soldiers. This is how Engel introduces his story:

> We are talking about a force that, since its arrival in Ramallah two weeks ago, has already combed through about half of the houses, and it's estimated another two weeks will be required to complete the procedure ... And we are talking ... about a very, very complicated action, because in spite of all the arms and means of combat, as well as the very substantial list of wanted people that have been arrested there, we are still talking about a town whose population, for the most part, consists of innocent citizens, so great care is required. And despite all this innocence, things can catch fire within a second, as you will now see.

The report itself starts with a long ride on an armored vehicle, along a Ramallah street. "In Ramallah", Engel dramatically announces, there's no one out on the street, but the street itself is shouting. Here, on Manara square, a month ago, the Palestinians hanged a collaborator. Along the streets, like endless wallpaper, hang [pictures of] *shaheeds* [martyrs], and a call to the remaining citizens to commit suicide by the same method. Everyone who has been involved in this is now hidden in these houses, if he hasn't been caught already ... Every house might hold a terrorist, but then again, it may just as well house an innocent family, that has nothing whatever to do with terrorism.

As the ride comes to an end, we now watch a group of soldiers knocking on one of the doors. "How do you feel about this?" asks Engel, and this time, unlike the report that incensed Defense Minister Ben Eliezer, the soldier answers as expected: "How do I feel about this? At first, you don't know what to expect, maybe they're getting ready there, you know. In the end you see this old guy, a human being after all – and you make the switch." And another soldier says: "Obviously the situation we're in when entering houses ... is not a simple situation for us either, but there's no other way to check. So we try to do it as politely as possible, with maximum alertness." When the soldiers, along with Engel and his camera, leave one of the apartments, the owners wave them goodbye (one of the women actually says "thank you").

Night comes, and Engel, his face lit up by a small torchlight in the dark of the street, says "In Ramallah, at night time, this can go on for hours. Moving from house to house ... only to go on to the next. But here, in Ramallah, it turns out, you never know what will happen the next minute, what's waiting around the next corner." Now, of course, we hear the shooting. The camera trembles. The soldiers shout, take cover, return fire. "In an area as densely populated as Ramallah," says Engel,

> even if the source of fire is identified, the shooter vanishes in seconds ... within a minute, the force will move into the building. Once they bring down the iron door, the house inside will already be empty. Those who fired the shots could be in any one of hundreds of other houses in the same neighborhood, mingling somewhere with the rest of the population.

This is the time for a critical question. "Do you ever think this activity is making people [here] much more militant?", Engel asks one of the soldiers, who answers "Very likely, we're not naive." And his friend quickly explains: "The difference between us and them is that every bullet we shoot, we only shoot at terrorists, not at innocent people."

The next morning, the soldiers let a Red Cross worker bring food to a local civilian, despite the fact that she had broken the curfew. And then, they keep on searching for one of their "wanted individuals", and eventually capture another suspect, who has hidden in a cupboard for two weeks, "with food and arms". "Shortly after this success," Engel concludes his report, "the curfew here will be lifted for four hours. Wanted people will use this opportunity to change their location and regroup, before another night of action in Ramallah."

There is nothing in this report which is not about the suppression of guilt: the soldiers' mission requires "great care" because "we are still talking about a town whose population, for the most part, consists of innocent citizens", yet "despite all this innocence, things can catch fire within a second". The soldiers are sensitive, they "make the switch" when they have to, because for them, too, "the situation is not simple". And indeed, they do let the Red Cross worker pass, even though she broke the curfew. And finally, when the curfew is lifted, the one result which Engel decides to highlight is that "the wanted people will use this opportunity to change their location". There is almost nothing in this report which is about operation Defensive Shield, as such, or about terrorism, or the fight against terrorism. It is all about the soldiers, as Israelis – they are determined, responsible, independent in their thinking, and, most importantly, morally sensitive.

On Channel 1, the overall perspective on April 12 is entirely different. Commentator Oded Granot, much calmer than Ehud Ya'ari, makes do with a matter-of-fact presentation of the Palestinian position:

> The official position states: We shall not torpedo Powell's visit, but under the surface all kinds of things are constantly being said with the purpose of explaining one thing: The rules of the game have changed. ... We must move on directly to a final status agreement, and first of all we must reach a situation in

which Israel withdraws from all the territories it has occupied, because it is unthinkable, for instance, that Arafat will declare any sort of ceasefire while the IDF is still in Ramallah.

Granot then broadcasts a short item about a UN food and medicine convoy, stopped by the IDF on its way to the Jenin refugee camp – the very camp which was then at the center of worldwide attention, and was not even *mentioned* throughout the entire edition on Channel 2. In the report, the UN spokesman in the West Bank says: "We are seeing a kind of humanitarian crisis in the Jenin refugee camp. We have tried to reach the camp and the *kasbah* several times … and it was canceled at the last moment. This has happened to us several times, and we are frustrated."

Next appears Ron Ben-Yishay, who explains (more or less like Ronny Daniel) that the IDF plans to stay in the area for a long time. A few minutes later, however, commentator Amnon Abramovitch says the following as a reply to a question posed by anchor Orit Lavi-Nesi'el:

Look Orit, I don't want to sound heretical, but let me tell you this: all the activity in the past year, and especially during operation Defensive Shield, has centered on the Palestinian Authority – not on Islamic Jihad, not on Hamas, who are the ones responsible for these terror attacks. The *Tanzim* joined them later, to maintain its status on the streets. But the *Tanzim*, and certainly the Authority, are our future partner. We are, to a large extent, injuring our future partner, but are leaving behind Hamas and Jihad – certainly in the Gaza Strip – and they are the ones who initiated all the violence against Israel. And really, what we have done there is create a state of chaos – we have damaged the computer network of their educational system and their citizens' register. The question now is who will manage the population there, and how? After all, this action must come to an end some day, and there is no way of knowing who will manage things, and how. So, when you ask what this action has achieved, I have no answer for you. Motivation has increased, of course; it exacts a certain human price on both sides, and, it should be remembered, there is an economic price as well.

The difference in perspective between these words and those of the commentaries on Channel 2 could hardly be more significant. Abramovitch reports the damage inflicted on the civilian infrastructure – an issue we shall return to shortly – and highlights the all-important fact that most of the IDF's action focused on the Palestinian Authority and not on the main terror organizations (thus completely contradicting the official position, represented by Udi Segal). Abramovitch explains that "we are, to a large extent, injuring our future partner", and, most importantly, he does not hide behind passive formulations like the ones used by Daniel. He clearly states: "What we have *done* there is create a state of chaos." All of which culminates, again, with a special report from the ground. This time, however, correspondent Gur Tsalal-Yachin brings in a real piece of investigative journalism, dealing with the IDF's attempt to "clean up" Jenin:

> Following the gun-fighting, in an almost secret operation, the IDF is now trying to fight for public opinion. The bodies of some Palestinian refugees have been lying in the camp area for many days. Please recall that in the course of this week soldiers who came out of Jenin reported that the camp's alleys were filled with the stench of bodies. Israel wants to prevent images like those shot this week in Nablus: Palestinian corpses concentrated on the streets of the town. The Palestinians have claimed that a massacre was taking place in Jenin and that IDF soldiers killed innocent people. Today, the head of military intelligence General Zeevi Farkash, says: That's propaganda. ... and Israel is trying to produce its own media spin. The IDF is preparing to collect the bodies almost secretly, the operation is supposed to be carried out far from the public eye and the TV cameras. And these, Orit, are the details that we are allowed to report tonight concerning the so-called "clean-up action" – within the limitations set for us. Last night lengthy discussions were held in various IDF headquarters, the medical command and the military rabbinate among others; guidelines were handed down and forensic specialists were quickly mobilized. Dentists, laboratory technicians and people at the military rabbinate who specialize in the identification of bodies were called up too. It's still unclear what will be done with the Palestinian corpses still buried under the rubble of Jenin refugee camp.

Some military sources have said that the Palestinians will be given another opportunity to collect those bodies they want to bury themselves – certainly civilians' bodies, if such are found. One possible negotiator, in such a case, would definitely be the Red Crescent, but the IDF is preparing for the option of burying the dead Palestinians at the terrorists' cemetery in the Jordan Valley – at least the bodies of wanted men. Special cooling vans are already on standby near Jenin, and that's where the bodies will be kept until there is a decision about what to do with them. No one knows for sure how many dead bodies there are in the area – how many are those of civilians, and how many of terrorists. The IDF, in any case, is preparing for anything between one hundred and three hundred bodies.

There is a world of difference between this special report and the one by Engel on Channel 2, and not just for the usual reasons – the fact, for example, that the IDF itself probably liked Engel's story much more than it liked Tsalal-Yachin's. The most important issue here is the very acknowledgment of the fact that the general context of both these special reports is the context of *public relations*, the context of the fight over self-image and the allocation of blame. Tsalal-Yachin does not only report something that simply happened on the ground, that is, the arrangements for the "clean-up" of Jenin; he quotes General Farkash as accusing the Palestinians of propaganda, and then explicitly states that Israel does the very same thing, that it was "trying to produce its own media spin". The first implication of all this is that the Palestinian claims are not necessarily false: as it turns out, the IDF itself is "preparing for anything between one hundred and three hundred bodies". The deeper implication has to do with the general context: in the fight over the allocation of blame, the Palestinians do not necessarily lie, and Israel does not necessarily tell the truth. Engel's story, on the other hand, does not acknowledge that its topic is actually that of the allocation of blame. It refrains from explicating the all-important fact that the question it attempts to answer – what are the soldiers in Ramallah actually doing? – has been asked all over the world, again and again, and has already received some very unpleasant answers. Engel does not acknowledge that these answers are hovering over his report, that his report, in other words, is in actual fact constructed (consciously or unconsciously) as a statement of defense against these answers. And through all this, of course, Engel maintains – reconstructs – the sense that his own report is exactly that: a *report*. He himself is only an observer, not someone who actively participates in the ongoing discourse of blame.

All this is significant enough, but there is another difference between the two reports which is even more important: Engel's report is explicitly about the soldiers, and about them as Israelis in battle, and is thus a statement about *us*, a statement which immediately implies that *we*, individual Israelis, have a stake in the fight over the allocation of blame. Tsalal-Yachin, on the other hand, explicitly states that his report is about Israel, as a *state*, and about the IDF, as an active *agent* on the ground, not about Israeli identity. Establishing the fact that Israel, as a state, is actively involved in a propaganda campaign, Tsalal-Yachin in effect releases *us* from the discourse of blame by separating Israeli identity from the identity of the state, and thus provides the basis for critical coverage.

5

"The Problem with Sharon's Plans": The Suppression of Intention

How, then, does the obsession with guilt translate into a world-view? What conception of reality do all the different media share, beyond the significant differences in their perspectives about the operation? What is it that makes the critical formulations we have looked at – the ones by Amnon Abramovitch and Gur Tsalal-Yachin on Channel 1, for example, or by Tsadok Yekhezkeli in *Yediot Ahronot* – seem so exceptional? Well, as we shall see in this chapter, the common denominator, the foundational basis, lies in the portrayal of Israel – its government, its military, its people – as an *agent without intentions*, an innocent society that has been pushed into the operation, just as it was pushed into the entire Intifada, by the sheer force of Palestinian violence, with no agenda of its own except self-defense. Operation Defensive Shield, in other words, is characterized by all news providers as nothing but a desperate attempt to do something – whatever possible – against terror. This is the shared foundation, and from here on, the positions vary: *Ma'ariv* staunchly supports the government and the military in this no-choice war, contributing to the effort in directly silencing critical questions and in publicly calling on the government to "crush" the "Arab dismal ritual of death". Channel 2 simply characterizes the operation as a reasonable activity against terror. *Yediot Ahronot*, *Ha'aretz* and Channel 1 are much more skeptical (some of the time) – but not with respect to the foundational principle. They all agree, in one way or the other, that Sharon's government was pushed into the operation by Palestinian terror, and when they do criticize the government, they chastise it for having no plan. "We are rolling into a war ... with no name and no aim", writes Nahum Barnea in his commentary in *Yediot Ahronot*, and Sever Plotsker writes in the same edition that Sharon's government, which is "characterized mainly by stagnation and fixation", is yet again brandishing the "weapon of reaction-retaliation". Yoel Marcus, in his article in *Ha'aretz*, says that "no country would tolerate a situation in which its capital, its cities and towns are the constant target of murderous attacks of the type inflicted on us by the Palestinians", and then cautiously proceeds to the issue of Sharon's so-called "unfolding operations". And Amnon Abramovitch and Oded Granot of Channel 1 constantly say that they would like to believe that Sharon actually has a "future political plan". What all these critical stands have in common is, quite simply, their portrayal of Sharon as a Prime Minister who does not know what he is doing.

The most remarkable feature of all the critical formulations, then, is that none of these commentators ever raises, or even hints at, the possibility that Sharon actually knows *very well* what he is doing, that he *does* have a plan, and that he is not particularly bothered by the fact that the military operation will not lead the parties back to the negotiating table. In other words, the media *never* formulate the alternative interpretation: that Sharon has not been passively pushed into this action by Palestinian terrorism – and that he is gaining political and diplomatic points (such as keeping the Labor Party in his coalition, and maintaining reasonable relations with the United States) by deliberately keeping his intentions unclear.

Is this alternative interpretation necessarily true? Not at all. But the reporters working for the five media institutions consistently brought in materials which strongly suggested that this interpretation may actually be closer to reality. These materials, however, were systematically published, or broadcast, in a way that amounted to suppression.

Thus, for example, senior reporter Ben Caspit, who regularly contributes to *Ma'ariv*'s front news pages, publishes a story in *Ma'ariv*'s Passover supplement, on April 2, about certain suspicions within Sharon's cabinet regarding his future plans. The plans, which were leaked to the press *weeks* before the operation, were supposed to include, first, an all-out war on terror, and then, at the second stage, a dramatic move towards peace. In the eighth paragraph of the report Caspit writes:

The problem with Sharon's plans is that they don't always look the same on the outside as they do from within. They often include both real and imaginary parts, intended to misinform and manipulate both political rivals and partners. And in the end, they usually go wrong. Shimon Peres' people, for instance, suspect that Sharon will perform the first part of the plan (painstakingly) – he will topple and wreck anything that can be toppled and wrecked – and will then forget the second part, which includes a generous and dramatic peace offer, the evacuation of settlements, and progress towards an agreement.

To be sure, suspicions of this type, arising within the government, touch on the very heart of the matter. From any reasonable point of view, they are worthy of a first-page headline. *Ma'ariv*, however, publishes them as far away as possible from the news pages – framing them as "background information" – and makes a point of reflecting a strong sense of unity and consensus on its front page. The result thus strongly indicates that as far as the paper is concerned – as far as the readers *should* be concerned – Caspit's story is not what it seems to be. It does not say something of significance about Sharon's intentions with respect to the operation, but rather about, say, the personal mistrust between the Prime Minister and his Foreign Minister. This, of course, could indeed have been a relevant interpretation of the story, if other suppressed reports did not indicate that the suspicions were probably founded. Here is another excerpt, again from an article by Ben Caspit, this time from *Ma'ariv*'s weekend supplement of April 5. The passage quotes sources from the Prime Minister's entourage:

"Israel has made some mistakes," they acknowledge, "in our time in office as well. We let the world get used to the fact that we are a reasonable, moderate, restrained country, able to take losses without reacting – a responsible country. Well, that's over and done with. No more. We are crazed now. Dear friends, please welcome Crazy Israel! It should be clear to everyone, that Israel is no longer a doormat, a victim, a silent victim. From now on, we'll screw anyone who hurts us. Palestinians crossing the line? We'll give it to them. Syrians crossing the border in Lebanon? We'll screw them. The Palestinian Authority turning into a terror factory? We'll exterminate it. From now on, these are the rules of the game. The only rules."

The materials suppressed by *Yediot Ahronot* take the entire story one step forward. They strongly indicate that Sharon does have a plan – one which is in no way limited to security issues – and that he is indeed actively interested in keeping his intentions unclear. Consider, for example, the following report by correspondent Ron Leshem, in the weekend supplement of April 5. Leshem, it should be noted, is published almost daily in the front news pages, and his stories there *always* focus on the glorification of the IDF soldiers' courage and dedication. In his April 5 report, under the title "It Won't End Without Gaza", Leshem writes:

> The messages which the General Staff is getting from the political echelons are vague and contradictory, and add up to an equation consisting mainly of question marks. The IDF is trying to cross this line on tiptoe – but running amok at the same time. It is moving ahead with blindfolded eyes, unable to get answers to the crucial questions: what is the ultimate goal? Will two weeks be allotted for the mission, or a half a year? What kind of reality should we expect at the other side of this adventure? ... If we totally wipe out the Palestinian security forces, say people in the IDF, who will do the dirty work after we leave? Crushing the Palestinian forces may force the IDF to stay on in the A areas for years.[1] This is why senior officers are worried about the Prime Minister's implicit intentions. "In the best case," says one of them, "Sharon wants to drag out the current interim stage, until Arafat is gone. In the worst case, he wants the total annulment of the Authority, going eight years back in time, and the renewal of military rule [of the territories]. We can't really read him, and we are getting no explanations."

There could hardly be a better indication that Sharon's plans may, yet again, include what Ben Caspit calls "real and imaginary parts, intended to misinform and manipulate both political rivals and partners". According to Leshem's report, senior sources within the IDF understand quite well what the implications of the operation will be – way beyond the fight against terrorism – and are actually worried and confused about the Prime Minister's "implicit intentions", which, as they explicitly say, go beyond the automatic response of "reaction-retaliation" – in *either* the best-case or the worst-case scenario. Together with Caspit's report, published on the same day, this story paints a picture of Sharon's goals and mode of operation which sharply contrasts with what the two papers highlight in their front pages.

Such indications reappear time and again in the reports sent in by *Yediot Ahronot*'s correspondents. The following paragraph appears in a report by the paper's Washington correspondent, Orly Azoulay-Katz, also published in the April 5 political supplement:

> US Secretary of State Colin Powell banged on the table and seemed about to lose it: "Sharon should be restrained," he told his senior advisers in a meeting at the State Department before the holidays. The images [coming in from the territories] were harrowing: the IDF laying siege to Arafat's headquarters, blowing up buildings, entering hospitals. Images shown on American TV, which might not be broadcast in Israel. Even the outrage felt by the American administration after the Passover eve massacre in Netanya has turned into fury with the Israeli Prime Minister. The documents piled up on Powell's desk, as well as Bush's, clearly prove that Sharon's moves do not prevent suicide attacks.

It turns out, then, that the US administration – along with at least one senior minister in Sharon's government and senior sources within the IDF – strongly doubts that Sharon's goals are confined to the prevention of terror. None of this, however, penetrates into the editorial text. When the administration reprimands *Arafat*, by the way, and expresses support for the operation, it does receive a front-page headline. Even more significantly, the paper also highlights the bold demand by President Bush to stop the operation, on its second week. What is suppressed, then, is not so much the fact that there might be disagreements between the US administration and the Israeli government, but the fact that senior members of this administration have a different perception regarding the possible intentions behind the operation.

Finally, it should be noted that about four months earlier, on December 14, 2001, in the same political supplement, *Yediot Ahronot* published a report by Alex Fishman, dealing with what was dubbed "the Dagan Plan". Under the headline "Sharon has Set the Trap, Arafat is Falling Into it", Fishman writes:

> None of the things that happened during the last days were accidental. It is all there, all written, in a document published at the time of the elections, under the title "the Dagan Plan" (named after (Res.) General Meir Dagan, Sharon's security adviser just before the elections, who has lately been appointed the head of the negotiating team with General Anthony Zinni). The plan reflects Sharon's world-view, which has two basic components, unaltered over the years. First, Arafat is a murderer, and one does not negotiate or do business with a murderer. Second, the Oslo agreement is the greatest disaster visited on the people of Israel in modern times, and thus, no effort should be spared in undoing it ... In the process of making Arafat irrelevant, says the plan, one of the first moves is to disconnect him from the people around him and from the Palestinian public ... Simultaneously, the plan is to cut up the Palestinian Authority into cantons, bits of territory isolated from each other, disconnected from any central government, and handled individually by Israel.

Moving on to *Ha'aretz*, it turns out, again, that some of the most important and significant factual statements – which in one way or another imply a different perspective regarding the question of intention – are systematically suppressed at the level of editorial text. The following examples appear in the reports by Aluf Benn (March 29), Amir Oren (March 31) and Ze'ev Schiff (March 31), but do not get mentioned in the headlines:

> The Prime Minister's associates mentioned yesterday that in the past Sharon has used "points of escalation" in order to step up Israel's response.

> [Major General Itzhak] Eytan finds himself, as usual, between the diplomatic hammer and the military anvil. He had no clear answers to the queries of commanders, who are worried about the excessive vagueness of their tasks, and he had to repeat the government's formulation – resulting from internal political compromise – which settled for defining Arafat as "an enemy".

This time, more than ever since the outburst of the military conflict with the Palestinians, Israel's military activity is accompanied by outrage over the terror attacks against Israeli citizens, running across the board from the senior command to the lower ranks. This is a major factor among the troops, and unless strict care is taken, it might affect events on the ground ... The precise objectives of the large-scale offensive – beyond the overall statement about "destroying the infrastructure of terror" – remain fuzzy even for senior ministers. The cabinet session which approved the offensive did not include, as is usual in such discussions, detailed maps and a list of the government's objectives, as well as the goals set for the IDF.

The point is that this precise situation – with Ariel Sharon obtaining the cabinet's support for a "major offensive", whose aims remain "fuzzy", without "detailed maps and a list of the government's objectives" – is one which veterans of the Israeli media, including most senior editors, should be more than familiar with: only twenty years have passed since the outbreak of the Lebanon war. Sharon, then Minister of Defense, managed to persuade his government, headed by Prime Minister Menachem Begin, to invade Lebanon for what he termed a "short-term operation", designed to destroy the infrastructure of the PLO (the Palestinian Liberation Organization) in southern Lebanon. In actual fact, his plan included the occupation of a major part of the country, with the long-term goal of changing the entire power structure in that fragile state. It took almost twenty years, and more than a thousand dead Israeli soldiers, before the IDF managed to leave the occupied country and pull back to the international border.

The similarity with the decision-making process at the beginning of that war, then, coupled with the different reports presented above – based mostly on Israeli, rather than foreign sources – draws a picture of the possible goals of the operation dramatically different from that which the papers themselves allude to at the level of the editorial text. There, the only two interpretative options accepted and highlighted are either self-defense, or no intention at all.

"THE COMMANDER'S SPIRIT":
BETWEEN INTENTIONS AND MISTAKES

The very same pattern characterizes the coverage of the IDF's actual conduct in the territories. The media do report Israeli actions which might be perceived as aggressive, immoral, unreasonable or unnecessary, but only to the extent that they do not imply prior intent at the senior military or the governmental echelons. In other words, the media report such actions only when they can be framed as "exceptions", or "mistakes".

Throughout the operation, for example, *Ma'ariv* shows no interest whatsoever in the Palestinian civilian population. It does, however, as we have seen, publish four items about suspected looting by individual soldiers, and one item about the suspected murder of a Palestinian by settlers. This is no coincidence: suspicions of this type, by their very definition, are about irregular behavior. Even the harshest critics of Israeli policy would not claim that the looting, for example, was directly planned by the state or the top military command. Thus, the publication of these cases by *Ma'ariv* only serves to confirm a double assumption: Israel, as such, is not involved in reprehensible activities of this type, and the Israeli media, playing its proper role in a democratic society, does not hesitate to report them openly and critically when they are performed by *individuals*. Even *Ha'aretz* and Channel 1, which in general terms position themselves on the more critical side of things, are careful not to cross the line when dealing with topics which might be considered test-cases for Israel's intentions. This is most clearly reflected in the coverage of two topics, which, from the point of view of the international press, were thought of as indicative of Israel's long-term intentions: the IDF attack on the Bituniya headquarters of Jibril Rajoub, the head of the PA preventive security in the West Bank, and the damage caused by the IDF to the civic infrastructure of the Palestinian Authority.

Throughout the Oslo years, Jibril Rajoub was considered by the Israeli military establishment as the most cooperative security official in the Palestinian Authority. Senior officers in the IDF have also publicly admitted that he was not involved in terror-related activities – before or after the outbreak of the Intifada. The attack on his headquarters, one of the highlights of operation Defensive Shield, was thus interpreted by some of the international press as evidence that Israel intended to destroy the Palestinian Authority *itself* – rather than wage war on those elements within the PA involved in terrorism. The massive damage inflicted on the civic infrastructure of the PA was also interpreted as prima facie evidence for this intent. *Ha'aretz*, then, just like all the other Israeli media, bases its coverage of the attack on the IDF's formal description of the event: the headquarters were attacked because wanted individuals found refuge there. *Ha'aretz*'s main headline on April 2 simply states: "Siege on Wanted Individuals at Rajoub's Headquarters; IDF Enters Bethlehem and Tul-Karem".

Crucially, this perspective is flatly contradicted in the commentary written by Danny Rubinstein, the paper's own senior commentator on Palestinian affairs, published on April 7 in section B of the paper – away from the news pages:

As far as we can judge at this point in time, of all the Authority's senior officials, Rajoub is the one who has paid the highest political price for this Intifada. This man – the most active partner in the security coordination with Israel, the one who would not let his people participate in terror attacks, the one who kept Hamas militants in jail – has been betrayed by Israel: in his wrecked and conquered headquarters the Israelis could get hold of wanted individuals from Hamas, thus presenting Rajoub as a collaborator in the eyes of the Palestinians. What happened at Rajoub's headquarters in Bituniya is the best indication of the operation's goal. The goal is the complete destruction of the Palestinian security system – so as to enable Israel to regain full military control of the West Bank. This is no scoop. In his election speeches more than a year ago, Sharon repeatedly explained that Israel's security cannot be left to the Palestinian Authority, which was later defined as supportive of terrorism and infected by it. And now the government, under Sharon's leadership, has made good on its promises: without Rajoub and his preventive security system there is hardly any Palestinian security system, and, in effect, no Palestinian government.

The same pattern can be detected in all the other media. On Channel 2, for example, reporter Yoram Binur goes out to the field and interviews Rajoub, who explicitly accuses Israel of betrayal after long years of cooperation. The interview, however, is broadcast towards the end of the edition, long after reporter Ronny Daniel and commentator Ehud Ya'ari discuss the issue in the studio. Daniel and Ya'ari tell the Rajoub story from the IDF's point of view, never even mentioning the fact the Palestinians have a different perspective on things – a perspective which is actually about to be presented, much later in the edition, by Binur.

In *Yediot Ahronot*'s political supplement, on April 26, senior correspondent Nahum Barnea publishes the following text – one of the most significant items of the entire operation:

> It is now admitted in Israel that Rajoub – whose nickname in happier times was "Gabriel Regev" – was the most moderate member of the Palestinian leadership, the only one who confronted Arafat and got a slap in the face and a pointed gun for his efforts. His organization was relatively free of involvement in terrorist activity. But the IDF got tired of him – tired of pseudo-prevention, of pseudo-arrests, tired of anyone associated with the Authority. The IDF made an omelet, and Rajoub was the egg broken in the process.
>
> And then there was the commander's spirit – the spirit of Sharon: the Palestinian Authority is an empire of terror and all its centers of powers should be annihilated, without asking too many questions about the day after. Concern about the day after is the hallmark of defeatism.

This passage is important not only because of what it contains, but also, and perhaps chiefly, for what it leaves out. True, says Barnea, Rajoub was the most moderate member of the Palestinian leadership, and true, there was that "commander's spirit", which maintained that "all ... centers of power" of the PA "should be annihilated" – and yet, all this notwithstanding, there was no *intentional planning*. "The IDF made an omelet," says Barnea, "and Rajoub was the egg broken in the process." And all this is the result of "tiredness", not the outcome of a plan. Barnea has all the information in this paragraph, but he simply avoids any mention of even the *possibility* that the action in Bituniya may reflect something deeper than an unintended consequence.

Note that the possibility of intentional planning does not necessarily imply that express orders were issued and delivered through the ranks, all the way from Sharon to the commanders in the field. Many of the people interviewed for this book, including senior correspondents, were under the impression that Sharon's "commander's spirit" did not translate into explicit orders given in formal briefings with the middle-ranging officers. The formal orders did indeed refer to "the infrastructure of terror". But Sharon's "commander's spirit", my interviewees estimated, deeply influenced the lower-level commanders and the soldiers, thus creating an atmosphere conducive, among other things, to the destruction of the civic infrastructure of the PA. In this sense, then, the entire system was indeed operating with a general sense of intention. This is how one of the senior military correspondents described circumstances in an interview:

> The atmosphere there was incensed and hot-blooded, and they did things there which should not have been done. I know the IDF commanders. There was no order, at any time or anywhere, for something systematic. But when the Prime Minister and Chief of Staff Mofaz talk as they do – *get rid of Arafat, they're all terrorists*, etc. – this trickles down, and when this happens on top of everything else, and the newspaper headlines, and Sharon and Mofaz stoking the fire – that's when you get many exceptions.

These comments are significant, mostly because none of this ever appeared in the Israeli media throughout the operation. In most reports, and, as we have seen, in all the reports highlighted by the editorial text, the soldiers are portrayed as sensitive, thoughtful and considerate towards the Palestinian civilians, and their state of mind is described as serious and not over-emotional. The possible link between Sharon's rhetorical style and the soldiers' conduct is never mentioned. Consequently, and quite unbelievably, only a single report throughout the operation takes the damage inflicted on the PA civil infrastructure as its topic. The report, published in *Ha'aretz* on April 24, was written, of course, by Amira Hass. Even this single story, however, should teach us something of importance about the general, implicit editorial policy shared by all media, that is, to downplay stories which might imply intentional planning. As we have already seen, *Ha'aretz* publishes news items dealing with human rights violations in the territories on a daily basis, but all of the stories published in the news pages (concerning, for example, shortages of food and medicine) are about incidents which do not suggest intention at the governmental level. It is significant, then, that the single story dealing with the civil infrastructure was relegated to section B. In the article, with the title "How the IDF Defeated the Economic and Computer Infrastructures in Ramallah", Amira Hass describes what the soldiers left behind in the Ramallah-based "Sky" advertising agency, whose manager, Tareq Abbas, is the son of Mahmud Abbas (Abu Mazen), who for a short time in 2003 served as the Palestinian Prime Minister and was elected as President in 2005 following the death of Yasser Arafat:

> Manager Tareq Abbas asks himself what happened to the ornamental wall at the entrance, which simply disappeared. The toilets are blocked and they stink. Damaged computers are thrown about, with broken disk drives. Hard disks have vanished. There was about $1000 in one drawer – the money has disappeared. A VCR is gone. Children's toys marketed by the firm were vandalized. All the visiting cards of clients and potential clients are gone. The soldiers have left behind loose pages from an English-language manual for snipers, sketches of grenade launchers and night-vision equipment. And one soldier, of Anglo-Saxon origin judging by his fluent English, has left a letter in Abu Mazen's son's office: "To all fucking supporters of terrorism, thanks for the coffee and the toilets. I hope you'll all die screaming and burning and go to hell." Similar or even worse scenes of devastation were to be found the day before yesterday in offices in Ramallah and El-Bireh (and in Nablus and Bethlehem) which IDF soldiers entered – at the Housing Bank, in the buildings of all the Palestinian Authority's offices (except for the Ministry of Planning, headed by Nabil Sha'ath, and the Sports and Youth Ministry). Their computers had been vandalized in various ways and documents were either torn up or missing.

This is the paper's *only* explicit reference to this critical issue throughout operation Defensive Shield. In the other media, apart from the few scattered remarks made by commentator Abramovich on Channel 1, the topic is never mentioned – as if it simply never happened.

"ARAFAT SHOWS NO SIGNS OF CRACKING":
FOLLOWING BARAK'S LEGACY

This foundational perspective, which refrains from ascribing Israel with any prior intent, perfectly fits the parallel perception of the *other* side which all the media project. If Israel is the passive entity, dragged into a war against its will, then the Palestinians (and most significantly, the Palestinian leadership) are always crystal clear about their goals, these goals are always totally evil, and whatever they do, their every action, always fully conveys their intentions. Needless to say, this perspective is most dramatically reflected in the portrayal of Yasser Arafat.

The attitude of the Israeli media towards the Palestinian leader can be summarized in a single word: admiration. Obviously, the media also project deep loathing, great fear and tremendous anger – but the end result, the type of character that emerges, is that of a sinister hero taken from the world of fantasy. Dozens of items published throughout the month focus on Arafat, and they all tell the story of a larger-than-life enemy: evil, murderous, cunning, subtle, determined, invincible. He is always in full control of the events in the territories, and even his isolation in his headquarters in Ramallah only strengthens him; the weaker he grows, the more powerful he becomes; he is absolutely invulnerable; he keeps on lying to everybody and betraying his own people, and, most importantly, he is simply enjoying every minute.

Thus, for example, a headline on page 5 of the March 31 edition of *Yediot Ahronot* proclaims "When the Stench of Death is in the Air, He Comes Fully to Life". Another headline on the opposite page adds: "Anything Goes – Except For Killing Arafat". The front page of the paper's weekend political supplement, two days earlier, announces: "Arafat is Not Depressed and Has Not Lost Control". A week later, on April 5, reporter Ronny Shaked publishes a story, in the same supplement, about Arafat's experience under siege. It is published under the headline: "A Living Shaheed", with the following subtitle:

> In spite of the siege, in spite of the distress, in spite of the psychological pressure, Arafat shows no signs of cracking. He controls his people and stays up to date from his Ramallah office. A *rais* [leader] in jail: what he eats, how he sleeps, who

is there with him, how he transmits his messages, how he intends to keep up the fight.

An identical story appears in *Ma'ariv* three days earlier, on April 2, under the headline "Die-Hard's Struggle for Survival", with the subtitle:

> Even though IDF soldiers are positioned right behind the door to his office, Arafat's sense of triumph is confirmed by the knowledge that his life is in no danger. His forced isolation brings back happy memories of his time in Beirut. Whether under siege or not, he goes on talking about his wish to be a *Shaheed*, and the message is quite clear to the youths standing in line to join the death March.

This goes on throughout the month, even in the most critical commentaries. As far as Arafat is concerned, no differences of opinion can be traced. Here, for example, is commentator Sever Plotsker, in *Yediot Ahronot*'s editorial of April 9, asking the government *not* to turn operation Defensive Shield into a "colonialist war", because this is exactly what Arafat is expecting. The title is "Don't Let the Serial Arsonist Win":

> Trapped in his dungeon in Ramallah, Arafat is now fighting the last battle for his political life. His troops are dwindling, his political world has collapsed and he has nothing left to lose. This is why he is more dangerous than ever ... In order to delay his demise, Arafat will not hesitate to set the entire Middle East on fire. Let it burn down, let it explode in Armageddon. ... And yet, nevertheless, Arafat could still win this battle, and rise back to his political life, like a phoenix ... Helpless Arafat will vanquish Israel if our government behaves foolishly, insensitively and arrogantly, ignoring the Palestinians' national self-respect, thus transforming operation Defensive Shield into a colonialist war. Yasser Arafat, the serial arsonist, is standing at the back door of Middle Eastern history, with a flaming torch in his hand. He believes in his ability to set a fire that will devour everything, leaving only the wasteland in which he flourishes. We can stop him, we can stop ourselves, from reaching this point.

On television, the obsession with Arafat is most clearly associated with Channel 2's senior commentator on Arab affairs, Ehud Ya'ari. Ya'ari's spends most of his time on screen talking about Arafat, his intentions, his plans, his most secret thoughts. When he talks about him, his body language reveals a real passion. His formulations are strong, colorful, almost poetic. Here are three examples, from the news editions on April 1, 5 and 14, respectively:

> Everyone around him is low, in a bad mood – and Arafat is in good spirits. He continues rejecting all the appeals to accept some sort of formulation, combining the original Tennet document and Zinni's most recent proposal. I have said this before, and will repeat it: Documents found there [in Arafat's headquarters] establish a direct link between Arafat and his very close associates, and all kinds of activities linked to the organization of terror.

> Zinni presented Arafat with the administration's demands – in writing: action rather than statements, and first of all, handing in wanted people – those who are with Arafat at the *muqata'a*, as well as the armed ones hiding out in the Church of Nativity, and of course, an unequivocal declaration regarding a ceasefire, and the repudiation of terror. For the time being, Arafat's answer is shrouded in veils of counter-demands.

> This is what Arafat told Powell, more or less: Israel's claims about the Authority's involvement in terror are fibs; all the published documents were false. I will do all I can to help you – but only within my abilities. And first of all: the IDF must retreat ... He presents Powell with evidence about the extent of the IDF massacre, as he calls it. The Americans let him voice his myriad complaints, but they make a point of the fact that throughout the entire conversation, Powell pushed towards a more practical line: a demand for immediate action, and explicit warnings that the end of the game is near.

This, then, is the crux of the analytical perspective projected by all the media: the entire Israeli–Palestinian conflict, in all its incredible complexity, entirely depends on the individual personality of Yasser Arafat. This is nothing less than a fixation. None of the media ever attempts to question it, and once the IDF enters the *muqata'a* they all full-heartedly participate in the celebration of incrimination: if Arafat is guilty, then *we* are innocent. No one in the media raises an eyebrow when IDF officers explain, matter-of-factly, that the search for incriminating evidence against Arafat is one of the main goals of the operation. Here, for example, is General Amos Gilad – then head of research in the IDF intelligence – talking live, in the studio, on the April 5 edition of Channel 1's evening news: "I believe that the IDF has already attained its objectives: first, it has been proven that Arafat actually did engage in terror, and second, terrorist capability has been directly stricken." As Gilad goes on to provide a portrait of Arafat, he sounds exactly like the descriptions we have seen before (and note the general's sympathy for the Palestinians' distress):

> It is my impression that Arafat will never agree to lay down the weapon of terrorism. There is no willingness on his part to fight terror. He is willing to do one thing only: to impose on Israel his approach to what he calls peace ... Arafat has a violent streak, it's in his blood ... The Palestinian people are presently suffering economic and social distress which touches one's heart, perhaps my own more than others' ... We are trying to take care of the Palestinian population ... Sometimes I think we are more sensitive to this population than Arafat and his people.[2]

From the second week of the operation to its end, the search for incriminating evidence against Arafat became, for all practical purposes, the real event to be covered by the media. Whenever some sort of "proof" was found for Arafat's involvement in terror, the finding was reported as no less than a victory. The IDF produced press releases, organized displays and press conferences – and the media published and broadcast as much of this as possible. Throughout the entire period, only two writers – reporter Akiva Eldar in *Ha'aretz*, and columnist B. Michael in *Yediot Ahronot* – took the trouble to examine critically the "proofs" supplied and displayed by the IDF. Their findings were published in section B of *Ha'aretz* and in the weekly magazine of *Yediot Ahronot*. No mention of them ever reached the news pages. Here is, first, a paragraph from Eldar's article, published on April 23, followed by a paragraph from Michael's piece, from April 26:

> Among the seized Palestinian documents, which are on display on the IDF's website and are currently being distributed to

foreign ministries over the world, is a letter written by the PA's Chief of General Intelligence in Tulkarem, Hamid al-Dardukh, to his commander, Tawfiq Tirawi. This letter is of special interest. Along with the original, written, of course, in Arabic, the IDF site offers a full English translation ... The original says that "a negative attitude towards the armed men has evolved in some of the security systems, sometimes leading to internal crisis and complete rupture of relations. All this is happening just when the perception of the armed Fatah men as staff members, and as supporters of the PA and its security systems, is collapsing." A look at the English version of this document reveals that the word "collapsing" has mysteriously disappeared. In the original document, the Tulkarem commander is describing the demise of this perception, but readers of the translation learn of an extremely close connection between armed Fatah people, who carry out the terror attacks, and the Authority and its security systems.

The entire website [of the IDF] looks as if the IDF spokesman was quite sure that no one would actually bother to look at the documents themselves, and people would be perfectly happy with the learned commentaries that he has prepared for them, supposedly on the basis of the seized documents. ... Was the *Tanzim*'s terror activity financed by the Authority? According to the commentary, yes. According to the documents, no. All the "financing documents" are in fact a collection of bitter complaints about the Authority's tight fist, and the fact that it does not provide the *Tanzim* with resources, coupled with envious comments about the affluent Hamas and Jihad members ... and veiled threats that if this financial drought continues, the members will defect to Jihad and Hamas. Did Arafat approve of money transfers to people involved in suicide attacks? Those who only check the pre-digested texts, are led to believe this was indeed the case. But whoever reads the texts themselves will not find a trace of evidence. All the documents in which Arafat approves miserly payments to Fatah and *Tanzim* men (a fact which in itself is about as shocking as the discovery that the head of a party approves payments to his party members) precede, by many months sometimes, the first suicide attack by the *Tanzim*.

Within this general framework, the media simply refrain from asking some of the most fundamental questions regarding the causes behind the reality of terror – not just the questions having to do with Arafat's political situation, the extent to which he really controls the events, or the tremendous political complexity of Palestinian society – but also the deeper causal questions, having to with the inseparable link between the suicide attacks and the occupation, the frustration and the suffering, the targeted killings by the IDF of Palestinian leaders, and the ongoing reality of closures and curfews. Whenever a reporter brings in important materials regarding these questions, it is buried deep in the back pages of the supplements, or broadcast in a way that neutralizes its meaning. Thus, for example, correspondent Ariela Ringel-Hoffman interviews experts on terror for a story published in the April 12 political supplement of *Yediot Ahronot*. One of the experts, (Res.) Lieutenant-Colonel Danny Reshef, a former intelligence officer, makes the following comment:

> The method of closures between and around cities is the root of all evil. It began with Ehud Barak and was meant as a response to terror activity at the rate of one incident per month, or every two weeks. Effectively, it has turned an entire population into one homogenous bloc which produces terror. Israel's effort to halt five suicide bombers has turned the lives of all the Palestinians into hell, and has produced 500 suicide bombers. The system of closures did not only humiliate these people and make their lives miserable, it prevented their preventive security services from carrying out their work.

This pattern is most clearly demonstrated in the suppression of the connection between Israel's policy of targeted killings and the involvement of the *Tanzim*'s leader, Marwan Barghouti, in terror activities. Military reporter Yoav Limor, who contributes to the news section of *Ma'ariv*'s pages on a daily basis, publishes a long article in the holiday supplement of April 2, titled "Thousands of Human Bombs Ticking Away at a Frightening Pace". Limor writes:

> Many people in the defense establishment now believe that Israel has played a considerable part in the fact that the *Tanzim* has joined the circle of suicide attacks. The assassinations

of its senior members – from Tabeth Tabeth to Ataf Abiath – generated a tremendous urge to respond with a hit at Israel's most vulnerable spot ... In private conversations, the Prime Minister and Minister of Defense have admitted that the execution of Ra'ad Carmi – carried out during a period of relative calm in the occupied territories – was a mistake, and possibly undermined an opportunity to achieve a ceasefire and return to political negotiations.

This all-important piece of information does not merit a headline, and does not appear in the news pages, not even when the *Tanzim* leader, Marwan Barghouti, is captured by the IDF, towards the end of the operation. All the media celebrate the event, and photographs of the handcuffed Palestinian leader dominate the front pages, but the following report, this time by Nahum Barnea in *Yediot Ahronot*, is again relegated to the political supplement (of April 19): "Barghouti was Carmi's patron. The list of terror attacks which the defense establishment has attributed to him directly indicates to what extent Carmi's assassination has been a watershed in Barghouti's involvement in terror."

The most significant chapter in this short story is written a week later, on April 28. On that day, as we have already seen, novelist-celebrity Irit Linor publishes an open letter to *Ha'aretz* – on the cover of *Ma'ariv*'s daily supplement. In the letter, Linor accuses *Ha'aretz* of adopting the Palestinian perspective on the conflict, and she ceremoniously declares that she intends to cancel her subscription to the paper. Linor is most infuriated by reporter Gideon Levy, who, for years, has been publishing a weekly column in *Ha'aretz*'s weekend supplement, highlighting the daily suffering of Palestinians under occupation. Among other things, Linor writes "When Gideon Levy accuses Israel of having transformed Marwan Barghouti from someone seeking peace into a suicide terror impresario, this analysis is about as logical as the claim that the terror wave of 9/11 was a conspiracy of the Mossad."

This, then, is the entire story in a nutshell: Gideon Levy's perspective can be easily rejected by the consensual reader, because he is personally identified with a certain political position. The all-important factual reports by Barnea and Limor, who cannot be so easily dismissed on political grounds, are buried deep inside their articles, with no headlines, and do not make it to the news pages. The end result: even when senior Israeli security sources openly admit that a causal connection could be detected between Israel's conduct and the continuation of terror, and even when three senior correspondents report this, this significant fact does not make it across the threshold of the editorial text – and does not leave a mark in the Israeli public's consciousness.

6
Manufacturing Identity:
Remarks Towards a Conclusion

Every critical analysis of the media eventually faces the challenge of explanation. What is the *function* of news bias? What does it do? How does it influence the public? What is it supposed to achieve? Most critical theories of the twentieth century have concentrated on different versions of what Noam Chomsky famously calls the "manufacture of consent": together with other means of symbolic power, news bias is used, either consciously or unconsciously, for the construction of a public opinion of the type that would serve the interests of the power elite. This is how Chomsky, together with Edward S. Herman, sum up their framework in the introduction to *Manufacturing Consent*:

> [The] propaganda model ... traces the routes by which money and power are able to filter out the news fit to print, marginalize dissent, and allow the government and dominant private interests to get their messages across to the public ... [The model] suggests a systematic and highly political dichotomization in news coverage based on serviceability to important domestic power interests. This should be observable in dichotomized choices of story and in the volume and quality of coverage ... Such dichotomization in the mass media is massive and systematic: Not only are choices for publicity and suppression comprehensible in terms of system advantage, but the modes of handling favored and inconvenient materials (placement, tone, context, fullness of treatment) differ in ways that serve political ends.[1]

This perspective has a lot to show for itself. The media in Western societies work within a complex system of structural constraints, which in many different ways influence what they eventually publish and what they suppress. These constraints include, among other things, the media establishments' business interests, their tangled relationships with other businesses, their competition with the other media, the fact that they rely mostly on advertisement for profit, and the fact that they depend on the government, the military and the economic leadership for their supply of news. These constraints assert themselves at almost every level, from the special relationships between reporters and their favorite sources, all the way up to the intricacies of editorial policy. Together, they set significant limits to what the media can do. All this can be easily detected in much of what we saw throughout this book.

This perspective, however, misses out on another essential element in this complex story, which I would like to highlight in the following concluding remarks. Characterizing the media as playing a subservient role *vis-à-vis* the establishment – a role determined, in Chomsky and Herman's words, by considerations of "serviceability" – the propaganda model fails to capture the all-important fact that the media have an *independent interest* in the maintenance of a certain type of autonomous relationship with the public, a relationship that *cannot* be explained away as a channel of propaganda between the establishment and the people, and cannot be functionally reduced to a means of marginalizing dissent.

This relationship is based on the fact that the media tacitly promise to reaffirm for their audiences what they already think about *themselves*, thus providing them with a much-needed sense of security in terms of their *social identity*. The media do this within the constraints set by the systems of power, but as far as this function *itself* is concerned, the media are significantly constrained by considerations of "serviceability" to their discourse with the public, not to the establishment. In this chapter, I will try to characterize this function, and claim that in performing this function the media mislead the public in ways that are tangential to the issues of consent and dissent. I will suggest that in operation Defensive Shield, the patterns of bias produced by the Israeli media have more to do with this side of story than with the need to service the interests of the establishment. As we shall see, understanding the bias in terms of identity construction – identity construction as such, not as a means for marginalizing dissent – will help us provide a more subtle explanation for the complex patterns of bias described throughout the book.

The approach to be sketched in this chapter starts with the acknowledgment that social identity – the sense of belonging to, and identifying with, a group of other individuals – is a necessary component of individual identity, and continues with the understanding that *acquiring* a sense of social identity in the context of modern societies is a much more complicated task than might be assumed. Social identity revolves to a large extent around questions of *knowledge* and *belief*, and, no less significantly, around questions of *meta-knowledge* and *meta-belief*. Belonging to a certain society, being identified with it, entails an understanding of what the *other members of the society* think, know and feel about things, not each of them as an individual, but all of them as a group: what do they know, or think they know, about their own society, about what is happening to it and what it is doing? What do they think about it? What do they think about their role as members of their society? What do they think about themselves as members of this society? To what extent do they identify with their political leadership? What do they feel they can unite around? What do they feel tears their society apart? What do they think about what other societies think about them? How much do they care? Who are they willing to listen to, inside and outside the group? Who do they trust? What do they fear? What do they hope for? How do they communicate about these issues? With whom are they willing to communicate about them? What would they agree to talk about? Which words would they choose to use? About what would they prefer to remain silent?

Having the answers for these questions is a precondition for the maintenance of social identity, and not having them effectively means losing sight of the group. This is true for every type of social grouping, and each individual, each of us, faces a multiplicity of such challenges. Every individual has to figure out what his or her family thinks and feels about itself (Are we a good family? Can we trust each other? What are we willing to argue about? What do we prefer not to talk about? How do we present ourselves to the world?); what his or her circle of friends thinks about itself; what the professional community the individual is involved with thinks about itself; and the people in their neighborhood; and the religious community; the ethnic group and the gender group; the social class and the society at large. Mastering this complexity is necessary for people's well-being. The system of social power

– the government, the business elite – obviously has a stake in molding this set of entangled social identities to fit its interests, but the very fact that social identity as such is a necessity cannot be simply explained away as the result of elite propaganda.

The danger of drifting away from the group, of losing sight of who I am as a member of a group, is all the more acute in modern societies, for two reasons. First, modern societies are characterized by a high rate of *change*. New things, situations, events occur every day, and they all present new questions, or new versions of old ones, which need to be answered – again, not just in the sense that each member of the group needs to figure out what he or she thinks about them (a complicated enough task as such), but in the sense that each member must figure out what the other members of the group think about them.

The second reason has to do with the very essence of modern societies as *imagined communities*: they are large aggregates of individuals who do not know each other personally, do not communicate with each other directly, but nevertheless share a sense of belonging, not just with those members of the community whom they happen to know (family members, friends and colleagues) but with all the other members, those whom they have never met. Social identity at the larger level is thus *imagined*, not in the sense that it is false (it is not), but in the sense that it is not directly experienced. In this circumstance, personal communication (with family members, friends and colleagues) is not enough to gauge the state of the group.

What people need in this state of affairs, then, is a means of symbolic mediation between them and their group, and this is exactly what the media implicitly promise to provide. They tell their customers about the news, those new events and developments which come up and raise new questions of perspective, and they tacitly guarantee to answer them in the way they are most likely to be answered by the other members of the group. Doing this, and doing it through editorial practices *which do not acknowledge that this is their function*, the media take advantage of a real vulnerability, a real need, in order to maintain their *own* power over the public – not necessarily to service that of the establishment.

This analytical framework assigns a very different meaning to the calculation of *rating*, or *distribution*. To maintain its own status *vis-à-vis* the public, each media institution must prove that it reflects the perspective of the imagined community it represents – and the only way this can be done effectively is through demonstrating that a large number of people do indeed choose to rely on the media institution for their supply of the news. In this sense, the modern media's obsession with ratings cannot be reduced to the capitalist logic of advertisement (although, of course, it *interacts* with it, and is influenced by it, in many fundamental ways). Because news coverage implicitly promises to reflect social identity, ratings are the very guarantee that the media indeed provide what they say they do.

In the default case, for most people, all this results in *persuasion by peer pressure*: the very assumption that most of those who at this very moment read the paper together with me *already* accept the perspective projected by the paper is a good enough reason for me to accept it too. At the very least, it entails that if I decide to maintain a different position from the one projected by the paper, I may have to consider seriously whether to share my views with the other members, or to keep them for myself.

This perspective on the way the media persuades by reflecting the general sentiment was most eloquently developed in the writings of Gabriel Tarde, one of the most important sociologists of nineteenth-century France, who deserves to be read much more closely by anyone who is interested in the media in modern times. Anticipating Benedict Anderson's *Imagined Communities*[2] by almost a century, Tarde writes in *The Public and the Crowd*:[3]

> ... not all communications from mind to mind, from soul to soul, are necessarily based on physical proximity. This condition is fulfilled less and less often in our civilized societies when *currents of opinion* take shape. It is not the meetings of men on the public street or in the public square that witness the birth and development of these kinds of social rivers, those great impulses which are presently overwhelming the hardest hearts and the most resistant minds ... these men do not come in contact, do not meet or hear each other; they are all sitting in their homes scattered over a vast territory, reading the same newspaper. What then is the bond between them? This bond lies in their simultaneous conviction or passion and in their awareness of sharing at the same time an idea or a wish with a

great number of other men. It suffices for a man to know this, even without seeing these others, to be influenced by them *en masse* and not just by the journalist.

The important thing to understand in all this is that the function of identity construction, and the type of influence associated with it, are not confined in any way to those processes of persuasion which the power elite is interested in. They are central in every process of group formation where all the members of the group cannot directly communicate with each other on a regular basis. They are as important in the construction of social dissent (that is, in the construction of *consent* within social groups which define themselves in terms of dissent *vis-à-vis* the dominant group) as they are in the construction of national identity. This is clearly evidenced, as James Curran shows in his seminal *Power without Responsibility*,[4] in the extremely important role played by newspapers in the development of working-class consciousness in Britain of the first half of the nineteenth century. As Curran shows, the capitalist system was quick to react and successfully halted this development, but the fact nevertheless remains that global working-class consciousness (global in the sense of wider than a few factories in a single town) could not have evolved without the construction of an imagined community of workers from many different places, without the reflection of the sense that other people, whom the reader does not know, share his perspective on life, his worries and hopes, and his fears. The same is true for the development of minority consciousness, feminist consciousness, gay consciousness, and so on.

Radical critiques usually ignore this side of things, mainly because it conflicts with a certain conception of *freedom*. From Plato to Chomsky, persuasion by peer pressure is thought of as a form of subjugation, and the quest for freedom entails an effort to release oneself from societal beliefs and develop an *independent* mode of thinking based on *reason*. In many important ways, of course, this is true. But the assumption that people only prefer to adopt societal beliefs *because* they are conditioned to do so by the power elite, that in conditions of real freedom they would engage in individualistic, rational thinking and ignore what the others think (unless what the others think formulates itself as a rational argument in a discourse governed by reason), does not have a lot to show for itself. More than anything else, it seems to imply that critical thinkers know that people, deep inside, know the truth about themselves (that by nature, they would want to be released from societal beliefs and think independently), whereas they, the people themselves, *think* that they know something completely different about themselves (that maintaining their sense of belonging is sometimes more important to them than the quest for rational integrity). This, to be sure, is not a very good starting-point for critical theorizing which attempts to take people into account.

When applied to the understanding of the media, this rationalist perspective quite obviously translates into an analysis that reduces the role of the media to the manufacture of consent: if people are by their nature rational individualists (an assumption which might or might *not* be true), and if rational thinking is the major tool people have at their disposal to free themselves from their social slavery (another assumption which is not necessarily true), then the dissemination of societal beliefs *as such* amounts to a means of subjugation.

If, however, the need for the symbolic mediation of social identity through societal beliefs is accepted as a real factor in the story – if the very fact that such mediation takes place cannot be explained away as a means of subjugation – then critical analysis can take as its target the specific *ways* in which this function is performed. The question then becomes: what *type* of social identity do the media project? What do they tell people about their own society, and, by implication, about themselves? Do the media do it in a *responsible* way? What is the impact of all this on the way the people deal with the reality around them? How does it effect the way the society runs its business? And, most importantly, do the media acknowledge to the public that this is indeed what they are doing?

Isolating these questions from the issue of manufacturing consent – not in the sense that manufacturing consent has nothing to do with them, but in the sense that they cannot be theoretically reduced to it – allows for a better understanding of the complexity we have seen in the different perspectives projected by the media during operation Defensive Shield. Think, for example, about *Ma'ariv* and *Yediot Ahronot*. What the two papers project throughout the operation is best understood as a certain collective sensibility – two very different collective sensibilities – around which their readers are invited to find their sense of togetherness. The two senses of togetherness which the papers offer their readers differ significantly in their attitude *vis-à-vis* the establishment.

Ma'ariv offers its readers the type of collective sensibility which includes, *among other things*, total support of the government. This call for support does not *determine* the overall perspective of the paper. It emerges *from* the perspective as one of its conclusions. What *Ma'ariv* is telling its readers is this: we have had enough. Things have gotten to the point where we must reconsider everything we have always thought about ourselves. Surely, we do not all agree on everything. We have our own "petty internal squabbles ... [about] the Saudi initiative, about the pros and cons of the separation fence, about withdrawal or retrenchment in the territories". This, however, is not the time for political debate and oppositionary statements. Now, "we must all come together to protect our very souls, to protect our lives, which have become so totally impossible". Now is the time for strong action and for *strong words*: we have to fight "the Arabs' dismal ritual of death ... to overpower it, crush it, demolish it". We cannot go on letting Arafat and his terrorists determine our destiny. We have to find courage in some of the old cultural resources we have neglected for a long time, the Zionist ideology of old times and our Jewish identity, and we can also learn something from the "great democracies like the United States and Britain" – we can "join hands in encouraging those who have to make the decisions as well as those who will have to carry them out". And most importantly, we have to regain our sense of pride: "Facing the waves of criticism to be expected from abroad – and from within Israel as well – the majority of Israelis may hold their heads up high and say that we shall go on resisting by force whoever tries to sow destruction and terror among us." True, "we can expect Israel to be internationally accused for its actions", but "before this begins, we should make it clear to the world and to ourselves" that we pay a "painful price for our insistence on fighting ethically".

There is a complex attitude in all this, which asserts itself not only in chief editor Dankner's explicit formulations, but in all the editorial practices employed by the paper's editors: the quotes from the Hagada which find their way to the front headlines; the suppression of oppositionary views, of doubts concerning the goal of the operation, and of any information pertaining to the Palestinian population; the dozens of headlines glorifying the ethical standards of the soldiers; the complaints about the foreign correspondents' coverage, and the direct attack on *Ha'aretz*. This complexity obviously involves a direct and explicit statement of support for the government, but it cannot be reduced to it. All the other statements involved in this complexity do not just provide the emotional background for the assertion of consent. The assertion is entangled in them, not vice versa.

The type of collective sensibility which *Yediot Ahronot* offers its readers, on the other hand, is significantly different. What *Yediot Ahronot* is telling its readers is this: we have reached a dead-end. Terror has gone "beyond the limits of our imagination", and Arafat is doing his best "to set the entire Middle East on fire". We may as well admit that life is unbearable: "This ominous feeling of a suffocating personal siege, of a panic-stricken public, of a country on the verge of the abyss, of a wavering government, of the whole-world-is-against-us – all this we have had ample opportunity to experience on the eve of the Six Day War." This does not bring back happy memories: "We are still eating the rotten fruits of that war, day and night, every day." And now, our government, led by a prime minister we do not particularly trust, again appeals to "the revenge-retaliation weapon, not because it is appropriate or effective, but because it is the only thing the ministers can agree on. As far as revenge is concerned, we do indeed have a national consensus." This is it, then: our men, our husbands and sons, are again going to war, "a war with no name and no aim". We must support them; we must give them our love, and hope for the best. And in all this, what we find most difficult, most insulting, is the fact that the world still accuses *us* of everything. We know: things are not always perfect, mistakes are being made. When you make an omelet, eggs are sometimes "broken in the process". In the general frame of things, this is not very important. But we can talk about it. If Yafa Yarkoni feels offended by some of the things we do in the territories, if she wants to say something about it, we shall listen to her. After all, she is not a politician. She is one of us. We do not think she should be scapegoated for that. But anybody who accuses us *from the outside*, anybody who thinks they can sit there, in Paris or the Hague, and *judge* us, should understand that none of what is happening is our fault. We hoped for peace, we offered everything, and Arafat just messed it all up.

Is this the type of perspective one would expect from a paper engaged in manufacturing consent? Well, it might be argued that it is, that the paper manufactures consent for the operation by presenting the public with a critical perspective of exactly the type that would, on the one hand, mask the intent of manufacturing consent, and, on the other hand, result in the type of consent that the establishment needs. This, however, is a very *sophisticated* type of deceit strategy, and the implicit assumption that this is indeed what is going on is what gives this type of theorizing the appearance of a "conspiracy theory". A much more reasonable hypothesis would be that *Yediot Ahronot* engages in the same type of project *Ma'ariv* is engaged in: both maintain their own imagined communities, and provide their readers with two very different collective sensibilities, two different senses of togetherness which their readers might identify with. Quite naturally, neither of these sensibilities is that of dissent, for the simple reason that the great majority of Israelis, the great majority of *people*, are not dissenters. (Journals of dissent, to be sure, do project a dissenting sensibility, for the simple reason that their readers *are* dissenters.)

There is, however, a much more important issue at stake. The fact that the two papers, together with *Ha'aretz* and both television channels, concentrate as they do on the issue of guilt, strongly indicates that the *third person* involved in the discourse between the media and the public is not the government, or the military, but the *outside world*. What all the media project, what they offer their audiences as a core marker of identity, is a pungent sense of insult (added to the injury of terror), a sense that the entire world directly blames us, the people, for things we are not guilty of. All the media, as we saw, suppress information that implies guilt, but this does not seem to be the real issue. The issue is that of the suppression of guilt *itself*, guilt as a threatening sensation, and the source of the threat, the blaming entity, can be detected on almost every page, in almost every edition. The fact of blame itself is not suppressed. It is systematically highlighted and accentuated. This is why the newspaper reports dedicated to the ICJ hearings are such a good example. They do not suppress the fact that the hearings are taking place, and they do not just announce the fact in their front-page headlines: they actually present a line of defense. *Yediot Ahronot*'s headline addresses the ICJ judges in an explicit plea for justice ("You Sit in Judgment – and I Bury a Husband"), and *Ma'ariv*'s headline invites its readers to replace the judges and judge for themselves ("You Be the Judges"). This is not a manipulation designed to produce a sense of support for the government. Quite sadly, this is a rather accurate reflection of general public sentiment. This is what Israeli society felt like during operation Defensive Shield. It would be a mistake to explain this away as propaganda.

What the media's obsession with guilt signals, then, is that the context in which they function is not the enclosed context of the nation-state, but the larger context of world opinion and global *identity politics*. In this context, the sensibility projected by the media is that of a local community embroiled in an ethnic struggle, rather than that of a national community involved in a national struggle. This, as we saw, is why Channel 1 does manage to produce a different type of television. Precisely because it is state-owned, precisely because it has developed a certain professional habitus before identity politics took over Israeli television (in the form of Channel 2), the channel is capable – not always, but from time to time – of providing coverage which is not directly and emotionally about *us*, but about the *news*. This, of course, should not be read as a call for the return of state-monopoly over the media. Channel 1 probably manages to do this exactly because it is the exception, not the rule. But when it produces that certain type of coverage, what characterizes the coverage is its ability to put a distance between the journalists, the object of their coverage, and the audience. Critical coverage is then about the object – the IDF, for example, in Tsalal-Yachin's story about the cover-up plan – not directly about us. This releases the coverage from the global discourse of blame.

From this point of view, the Israeli perception of the conflict with the Palestinians should not just be thought of in terms of the struggle over the control of the land and the question of personal security. It is first and foremost a struggle over narratives and over justice, a struggle in which neither side attempts to persuade the other, but both sides desperately attempt to persuade the outside world. The Palestinians, quite obviously, feel that Israel has the upper hand in all this. It is important to understand that Israelis have a very similar feeling. The envy of the "highly refined Palestinian diplomacy", mentioned briefly in Chapter 2, is no manipulation. This is a real element in the story. The obsession with guilt prevents Israeli society from developing an alternative discourse, one which centers on the notion of *responsibility*, a discourse which rather than center on the struggle between narratives, not on the question of justice, bases itself on the simple understanding that at the moment, regardless of the historical causes, regardless of the different perceptions of "the origins of the conflict", the Palestinians are under Israeli occupation and not the other way around.

The fact that in all this the media reflect a public sentiment rather than manipulate the public towards consent, however, does not mean that no *deception* is involved. The media do deceive the public, and the deception is rooted in the fundamental fact demonstrated throughout this book: the fact that the editorial texts produced by the media as reflections of public sentiment do not *emerge from* the reports of the media's own correspondents, but rather *impose themselves on them*. The media, of course, do not acknowledge that. What they do is send their audiences two different messages at two different levels. At the declarative level, they deny that they provide them with a perspective designed to reflect what they already think and feel. They tell their audiences that they provide them with the *news*. (This is why, at the declarative level, most Israelis say that as far as they are concerned, the media are *too* liberal.) At the tacit level, however, they do signal to their audiences that they provide them with an *Israeli* perspective (which most Israelis, including those who declaratively complain about the media, manage to identify with), but here they deny that this perspective is simply an *opinion*. They insist that the perspective emerges from a certain *perception of reality*. This is evidenced most clearly in the fact that the media consistently advise their audiences not to listen to what the foreign correspondents have to say. The foreign correspondents, they say, are hostile witnesses (*Ma'ariv* says, of course, that Amira Hass is also a hostile witness). What they signal by this is a very simple message: we, the Israeli media, have sent our *own* reporters to the field, *and what they saw there was completely different.* As we saw throughout this book, however, these Israeli correspondents, most of whom are quite conservative in their politics, brought in an accumulated perspective not very different from that of the foreign media. The element of deception, then, does not reveal itself in the fact that the perspective reflected in the editorial texts does not fit a certain supposedly objective description of reality. It reveals itself in the fact that in order to reflect a sense of togetherness for their audiences, the editors had to ignore, push aside, suppress, much of the material that their own reporters brought in to the news desk and that they themselves *published.*

This, unfortunately, is most clearly demonstrated in *Ha'aretz.* When Amira Hass brings in her chilling testimony from Jenin, for example, the paper relegates the report to section B, thus implicitly accepting *Ma'ariv*'s contention that she is not one of *us.* Then, it publishes an editorial which starts by announcing that "correspondent Amira Hass spent a few days in the camp, and brought in an extensive article, published in this issue", and then goes on to assert that Hass's report somehow proves that "the Palestinian propaganda has made despicable use of unfounded tales ... in order to fuel hatred against Israel". The paper does not just dedicate its editorial to the suppression of guilt. It also uses Hass's report as a cover: the notion that the Palestinians spread propaganda in order to "fuel hatred against Israel" is not our opinion, and we do not just reflect our readers' perspective. This notion emerges from Hass's investigations on the ground. In this sense, *Ha'aretz* editors mislead their readers in a very fundamental way. The same observation applies, of course, to all the other media.

This fact, and the fact that media do all this exactly in order to maintain their relationships with their audiences, that they deceive their audiences *in order to maintain their trust,* implies a harsher critical judgment of the media than the propaganda model allows for: concentrating on the media's subservient role, the propaganda model implicitly implies that at the bottom line, the media cannot be held accountable for what they do, because they do, more or less, what they are told to do, what they have no choice but to do. Understanding that the media are engaged in their own independent project in this story, that they deceive the public by systematically reifying the public perspective, by turning the existing opinion into fact, provides a sound basis for the critique of the media. Independence, from its very foundation, entails responsibility.

Notes

CHAPTER 1

1. Dror Feiler, an Israeli living in Stockholm, exhibited an installation in the Museum of History in Stockholm, featuring a large basin filled with red liquid, with a small boat carrying the picture of a female suicide bomber, who killed 22 people in Haifa. The installation was vandalized by Zvi Mazel, the Israeli ambassador to Sweden, when he visited the museum in January 2004.

2. ZAKA (The Organization for the Identification of Disaster Victims) is staffed almost entirely by members of Israel's Jewish Orthodox community. The organization, founded in 1995, specializes in collecting and identifying bodies and their parts after terror attacks.

3. Some background: the second Palestinian uprising, known as *Intifadat Al-Aqsa*, broke out on September 29, 2000, following Ariel Sharon's provocative visit to *Harem el-Sharif* (Temple Mount), on the previous day. Sharon was then head of the opposition to Ehud Barak's government. Two-and-a-half months before, on July 11, Ehud Barak and Yasser Arafat, the Chairman of the Palestinian Authority, met in Camp David for what was supposed to be the final round of negotiations towards a permanent agreement between the two sides. The summit failed. Later on, at the onset of the Intifada, Ehud Barak claimed that in Camp David he made a very "generous offer" to Arafat (in terms of the conditions of the permanent agreement, especially regarding the size and borders of the future Palestinian state), an offer which, according to Barak, was flatly "rejected" by Arafat. Barak also accused Arafat of planning and initiating the Intifada, thus "proving", both in Camp David and on the ground, that the Palestinian leadership is not "ready for peace". This contention quickly became the backbone of a new political consensus in Israeli society, a consensus which seemingly obliterated the gap between right wing and moderate left wing: the traditional ideological debate centered on whether or not Israel should withdraw from the territories in exchange for peace. Since the outburst of the Intifada it "turned out", so to speak, that the logical foundation of the debate was wrong: Barak's government offered to withdraw, and the Palestinians rejected the offer, which implies that peace does not depend on anything Israel could do. The Palestinians are simply not interested in peaceful solutions. More than anything else, it was this consensual perception which paved the way for Ariel Sharon's victory over Barak in the February 2001 elections, and the general sense of support for his policies ever since.

   As we shall see, the Israeli media played a crucial role in the dissemination of Barak's narrative, even when their own reporters brought in significant materials which strongly indicated that Barak's offers in Camp David were not as "generous" as he described them; that the Israelis, the Palestinians *and the Americans* were equally responsible for the failure in Camp David;

and that the outbreak of the Intifada was a spontaneous outburst of anger and frustration, ignited by Sharon's visit to *Harem el-Sharif*, but at a deeper level generated by the long stalemate in the Oslo process. Equally ignored was the fundamental fact (almost totally suppressed in the Israeli media) that throughout the process, since its inception in 1993, the majority of the Palestinians were left under Israeli occupation and could see no real change on the ground which could indicate that the process might end up with a viable and independent Palestinian state. Virtually all the academic research done in the last four years on these topics seems to support these contentions, in direct opposition to what the great majority of Jewish Israelis still believe.

The Intifada, then, began with a massive demonstration at *Harem el-Sharif*, and it quickly spread throughout the occupied territories, and, for a limited amount of time, in many of the Palestinian towns within the 1967 borders. Despite a few half-hearted attempts to reach a ceasefire, the Intifada gradually deteriorated into a full-fledged war of attrition, taking place mostly in and around the homes of 3 million Palestinians, but also taking its toll on the Israeli side. From the outburst of the Intifada until July 2004, more than 2,500 Palestinians and more than a thousand Israelis have been killed. The great majority of Israelis were killed in suicide bombings, which reached their peak in March 2002, just before operation Defensive Shield.

4. *Yediot Ahronot* is by far the most popular newspaper in Israel. According to estimates, it reaches three-quarters of all Israeli households. Published in tabloid form, its daily editions comprise 60 to 100 pages in several sections: the news section, a daily supplement containing additional news, op-ed articles, feature articles and culture and entertainment columns, a financial supplement, a sports supplement, and two major weekend supplements. Despite its superficial resemblance to classical tabloids, *Yediot Ahronot* is a crossbreed. Like classical tabloids, it does include extensive crime reports and "soft news", but these usually appear towards the end of the news section. The front pages are dedicated to political and national issues – and the paper employs some of Israel's most distinguished political and military reporters and analysts. It is owned by the Moses family, which also owns 17 local newspapers, five periodicals and a publishing house, and is a senior partner in a television franchise holder, a cable television operator and a recording company.

Ma'ariv is the second most popular paper in Israel. It has been competing fiercely with *Yediot Ahronot* for 50 years, and in the last decade or so has adopted a strategy of similarity. In terms of format, graphic design, colors and photographs, the two papers are almost indistinguishable. In terms of content and perspective, for a long time they projected a very similar world-view. However, in operation Defensive Shield, as we shall see, they significantly parted ways. *Ma'ariv* is owned by the Nimrodi family, which also owns local newspapers, three periodicals, a publishing house and a recording company, and is a senior partner in a television franchise holder and a cable television operator.

The third paper, *Ha'aretz*, is probably the best known outside Israel, not just because of its English edition, but also because of its prestige. Owned by yet another powerful business family, the Schockens, its status resembles that of elite publications such as the *New York Times*. The paper enjoys broad distribution among senior officials, intellectual circles and the business community, which accords it an influence that exceeds the scope of its circulation. The Schocken family also owns 14 local newspapers and a publishing house.

Channel 1 is the government-controlled television station, also known as ITV (Israeli Television). Since its first experimental broadcasts in 1968, until 1993, when regular commercial broadcasts were introduced, it had a broadcasting monopoly in Israel. Channel 2 was the first commercial channel to broadcast in the new multichannel broadcasting environment after 1993. Although at the time Channel 1 experienced a certain identity crisis, and even though it is still formally free of rating considerations (as it does not air commercials), its broadcasts gradually grew to resemble those of Channel 2. As we shall see, the fact that it is directly controlled by the government does not necessarily entail a more pro-government coverage than that of its commercial rival.

CHAPTER 2

1. *Bad News fom Israel*, the study by Greg Philo and Mike Berry on the British coverage of the Intifada (London: Pluto Press, 2004), provides an interesting example. The authors spend a lot of time presenting the two conflicting narratives of the conflict, thus explicitly accepting the idea that no description of the conflict is simply *true*. However, when they discuss their audience study results they say, for example, that "the majority also had no knowledge of the link between the wars of 1948 and 1967 – that Palestinians who were displaced from what became Israel in 1948 moved to areas such as Gaza, the West Bank of the Jordan and East Jerusalem and were then subject to military occupation after 1967." As the authors report, "in the focus groups, the moderator was sometimes asked by the participants about the origins of the conflict. In response they were given a very brief account of the events of 1948 and 1967, based on the work of the Israeli historian Avi Shlaim." All this, to be sure, is a totally *factual* reference to historical points which are only relevant within one narrative, the Palestinian one. The two wars would not be described by anyone subscribing to the Israeli narrative as the "origins of the conflict", and the connection between the two wars would definitely not be thought of in terms of the Israeli–Palestinian conflict – it would center on the conflict between Israel and the *Arab states*. The Israeli narrative does not accept that Palestinians were displaced in 1948 (according to the narrative, they "left", or "ran away"), and Avi Shlaim is one of the Israeli historians whom no one subscribing to the Israeli narrative would even consider acknowledging. It should be obvious, or at least I hope it would be, that I generally accept the Palestinian narrative of the conflict, that I do think, for example, that in certain significant ways, although not in all, the deportation of Palestinians in 1948 and the occupation of 1967 do constitute the "origins of the conflict". The point here is not historical, but epistemic: whether we believe it or not, the Palestinian narrative cannot

be used as the factual basis against which media representations of the conflict are compared.

2. State-imposed censorship, and overt cooperation with the government, used to play a much more significant role in the conduct of the media in the first two decades following the establishment of the state in 1948. Not unlike the Palestinian media, or the media working in other contexts of state-formation, the Israeli media in the first decades were tightly controlled by the government and the different political parties, and it readily accepted forms of direction and censorship, such as the *editors' committee*, which systematically allowed the establishment to share information with the chief editors of the different media in exchange for an obligation not to publish. In one of its most important decisions, the editors' committee agreed to accept the constraints imposed on it by the military censorship, and to accept the establishment's demand to accredit military reporters. Since the 1970s, things have gradually changed. In many ways, such as the privatization of the media and the death of party-aligned newspapers, the changes resembled similar patterns in Europe. At the local level, the most important point of change was the 1973 war, which was followed by soul-searching among media professionals with respect to the role they had played before the war in the dissemination of the establishment's false conceptions about the possibility of a war. The victory of the Likud Party in the elections of 1977, and the peace agreement with Egypt in 1979, also contributed to the change. Since then, the Israeli media have regularly projected a much more complicated view of reality and of themselves, which, first, accepts in the great majority of cases the perspective of the establishment with respect to the conflict, but also makes an effort to project an image of the media as free and critical. The editors' committee no longer exists, and the role of the military censorship has diminished considerably, but the media, in most cases, accept a set of unwritten rules of self-censorship, a set of rules which asserts itself much less in terms of *publication* vs. *suppression*, and much more, as we shall see, in terms of *editorial practices*. This line of conduct cannot simply be explained as a continuation of the older policy through other means: it has much more to do with the construction and maintenance of collective identity, a role which the media perform in many ways independently of the establishment.

3. Pierre Bourdieu, *Outline of a Theory of Practice* (Cambridge University Press, 1977).

4. Dan Sperber and Dierdre Wilson, *Relevance: Communication and Cognition* (Oxford: Blackwell, 1986, 1995).

5. Daniel Dor, *Intifada Hits the Headlines: How the Israeli Media Misreported the Second Palestinian Uprising* (Indiana University Press, 2004).

CHAPTER 3

1. All this, quite clearly, closely resembles the differences between the coverage of the wars in Afghanistan and Iraq by the US and the Arab media, although the differences between the strategies adopted by the IDF and the US military with respect to the media are also significant. Most

importantly, the American military adopted a strategy of "embedding" reporters within its units, thus allowing the media to present their consumers with what seemed like genuine live coverage from the field, live coverage whose contents were nevertheless strictly controlled by the military authorities. The Israeli media, totally unreflective about their own conduct, were quick to recognize that control, and quite a few reports were published at the time which harshly criticized the US media.

2. Do the foreign reporters, and their editors at home, provide an "objective" coverage of the Intifada? Of course not. Many media (especially in Europe) observe the events from a perspective that seems to favor the Palestinian side. Many others (in the US for instance) carry reports which favor Israel. The point is that Israeli outrage against the foreign media goes beyond mere criticism of this or that instance of reporting or the general nature of the coverage – it reflects a general sense that "the entire world is against us", thus perpetuating the sense of siege felt by many members of the public, and adding an important factor to the general sense of despair. The saddest expression of this phenomenon was the call to put a stop to CNN broadcasts on Israeli television. Of all the international media outlets, CNN was remarkable in its strongly pro-Israeli bias, from the beginning of the Intifada in 2000 and even more so after September 11, 2001. The fact that the Israeli public failed to perceive this is perhaps the best indication of its psychological state. The contribution of the media to this rampant sense of injury is of course substantial. More on this, later.

3. The fifth item is written by Arie Eldar, a right-wing commentator who, significantly, is not a regular contributor to the paper. In his commentary, he engages in a dialogue with God, telling him about the Passover celebration which ended up with the terror attack in Netanya, comparing the event to the persecution of the Jews by the Spanish Inquisition.

4. It should be noted that opinions about Yekhezkeli's work differ within the Israeli media community. Some of the journalists I interviewed for this book argued that Yekhezkeli had not really been to all the places he claimed to have covered. Yekhezkeli's response was unequivocal: he invited these critics to identify themselves, so that he could sue them for slander. In any case, the differences between Yekhezkeli's materials and those sent in by other correspondents speak for themselves.

5. Readers who are familiar with the English edition of *Ha'aretz* should be warned that the following analysis applies to the Hebrew edition, the one which addresses the Israeli public. In the English edition, which addresses a totally different audience, some of the editorial patterns are significantly different. Thus, for example, in the English edition, the materials sent in by Amira Hass and other reporters about the Palestinian population are *not* pushed to the back pages, and the entire perspective corresponds much more closely to how the paper says it regards itself, that is, generally speaking, liberal, critical and oppositional. To be sure, this discrepancy between the two editions is exactly what the theoretical pespective developed in this book predicts: the two editions use the same reports (in translated form, of course) written by the same reporters. The two editions, however, are edited by two different editorial teams, with two different agendas, targeting two different audiences. The two agendas are thus implemented by editorial means alone: headline formulation,

allocation of space, distribution of materials across pages, and visual semiotics. The results are, quite simply, two different newspapers.

CHAPTER 4

1. In this respect, Channel 2 is a shade more generous than Channel 1. Thus, for example, when Prime Minister Sharon delivers his speech to the nation on March 31, MK Yossi Sarid, then head of opposition, is invited to the Channel 2 studio, and is asked for his response. On other occasions, he is allotted a moment or two to clarify his position, and a few other opposition MKs are fortunate enough to get occasional exposure. Channel 1, on the other hand, invites MK Sarid for a one-minute interview on March 29, and acquits itself of representing the opposition throughout the entire operation by inserting a sentence or two from an opposition member into this or that report, every few days, often framed by a sarcastic remark by the reporter or the anchor.
2. From time to time, the two channels invite special guests to the studio – mainly retired generals. Interestingly, the generals, who represent the military establishment, maintain the opposite division of labor. (Res.) Generals Yossi Peled and Shlomo Arad, who appear on Channel 1 on March 29, give the IDF full license to topple the Palestinian Authority, and categorically refuse to engage in any critical discussion of the operation's goals. "It's time we all understood that we no longer are in the right-wrong mode," Peled announces, "we are now in survival mode." On Channel 2, on the other hand, the one speaker who seems to bring a calmer mood to the studio is (Res.) General Danny Rothschild. In the following excerpt, Rothschild actually takes a much more moderate stand than anchor Haimovitch (and note, again, how Haimovitch starts out the discussion by representing "the people"):

Haimovitch: ... People feel that the effect of this attack [in Netanya] is such that this can't go on, you know, not the restraint, and most definitely not those same actions that have already been taken. So what can be done now?
Rothschild: This is exactly the question everyone should ask themselves. Look, to begin with, what really strikes me is that none of our leaders is addressing the public. ... But beyond this, the cabinet will convene today, there's nothing new and I am willing to bet that ... the people they're searching for, those who initiate the terror attacks, ... are already not where they were yesterday ... We have already been in all the places we are about to enter now, and the problem in these cases is that you know how you get in, but you don't know what will happen within an hour, or two hours, ten hours, twenty-four hours.

CHAPTER 5

1. The areas within the Palestinian territories which came under the Palestinian Authority's security responsibility as part of the Oslo agreements.

2. In June 2004, senior reporter Akiva Eldar published a special report in *Ha'aretz*, which exposed the exceptional and questionable role that General Amos Gilad played in the establishment of the Israeli intelligence evaluation that Arafat "will never agree to lay down the weapon of terrorism". Based on the testimonies of senior members of the intelligence community in Israel, including (Res.) Colonel Efraim Lavie, who at the beginning of the Intifada served as the Head of the Palestinian Desk in the IDF intelligence, Eldar showed that Gilad's assessments were *not* based on the Palestinian Desk's professional evaluations. As it turns out, these evaluations were quite similar to the reports brought in to the newspapers' news desk during the first week of the Intifada, which strongly indicated that Arafat's role in the outbreak of the Intifada was mush less significant than claimed by Ehud Barak, then Prime Minister (for more on this, see my *Intifada Hits the Headlines*).

CHAPTER 6

1. Edward S. Herman and Noam Chomsky, *Manufacturing Consent* (Pantheon Books, 1988).
2. Benedict Anderson, *Imagined Communities* (London: Verso, 1991).
3. In: Gabriel de Tarde, *On Communication and Social Influence: Selected Papers* (University of Chicago Press, 1969).
4. James Curran and Jane Seaton, *Power without Responsibility: Press and Broadcasting in Britain* (Routledge, 1997).

Index